SNAP

Making the Most
of First Impressions,
Body Language & Charisma

PATTI WOOD

New World Library
Novato, California

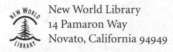

New World Library
14 Pamaron Way
Novato, California 94949

Portions of the section "Hands and Gestures," found in chapter 10, appeared in slightly different form in *Paid to Speak*. Copyright © 2011 by the National Speakers Association. Used with permission.

The material in this book is intended for education. No expressed or implied guarantee as to the effects of the use of the recommendations can be given nor liability taken. The author's experiences used as examples throughout this book are true, although in some cases identifying details such as name and location have been changed to protect the privacy of others.

Text design by Tona Pearce Myers

Library of Congress Cataloging-in-Publication Data
Wood, Patti, date.
 Snap : making the most of first impressions, body language, and charisma / Patti Wood.
    p.   cm.
Includes bibliographical references and index.
ISBN 978-1-57731-939-9 (pbk. : alk. paper)
1. Self-presentation. 2. Impression formation (Psychology) 3. Body language.
4. Interpersonal relations. 5. Social perception. I. Title.
BF697.5.S44W66 2012
153.6—dc23   2012021384

First printing, October 2012
ISBN 978-1-57731-939-9
Printed in the USA on 100% postconsumer-waste recycled paper

New World Library is proud to be a Gold Certified Environmentally Responsible Publisher. Publisher certification awarded by Green Press Initiative. www.greenpressinitiative.org

10 9 8 7 6 5 4 3

For Roy

CONTENTS

INTRODUCTION

What do people think of you when they first meet you? Everyone forms first impressions all the time — the new team member you met in the break room, the prospect you're selling to, the woman interviewing you for a job, the online dating match you just connected with, the conference room full of people you just presented to. How can you improve the impression you make?

How do you feel about your ability to form accurate first impressions of others? How do you know if you can trust a person you've just met to be a good manager, employee, business partner, or friend; refinance your mortgage; or provide care for your toddler or parent? Are you good at reading people? Is your gut reaction accurate?

This book addresses all these questions and many more.

If you've ever wondered why you didn't get a callback after you thought you'd aced an interview, or wondered how a business contact could go wrong, how a "friend" could turn out to be untrustworthy, or how you could feel an instant connection to someone you've just met, I'll help you understand why.

Even after years of studying, speaking, and consulting on

these processes, they still leave me with a sense of awe. It's astonishing, but research shows that when making a new contact, we decide if we like someone — and people do the same with us — within a *fraction* of a second. These are snap impressions. They are quick, powerful, and surprisingly accurate. We're hardwired to give and receive them.

You might say, "That's not enough time, I don't make a good first impression, that's not fair, I don't do that," but when you understand how snap impressions work — the factors that form them and the hundreds of nonverbal cues hidden between a hello and a handshake — you will see that snap impressions are not *snap judgments*. The latter are influenced by attraction, stereotypes, deception, communication styles, and habits that wreak havoc with our ability to read — and be read — accurately.

Snap impressions, on the other hand, give you an internal rudder, a map to the treasure of each person's true self. Because we can process thousands of units of nonverbal information in less than a minute of contact, nonverbal communication can help keep us where we need to be and with whom. And because nonverbal signals are usually not under an individual's conscious control, they are more honest and revealing than words.

Best of all, we can *learn* to read body language skillfully. Snap technology is something you can practice and master. As you do, you improve your ability to give and receive impressions accurately, and your personal and professional relationships become more genuine, productive, and successful.

I believe that the greatest gift we can give other people is to truly understand them, to really see them. And that one of the greatest feelings we can experience is that of being truly understood and seen.

—⁂—

I came into this world as a result of the power of snap impressions. Before my mother was my mother, she went out dancing one evening, spied a cute blond man across the dance floor, opened up her heart, and thought, "That's him." My future father looked across the same dance floor, saw a cute blonde woman, opened up his heart, and thought, "That's her."

"Thought" isn't really accurate, since the cues our limbic brain (the system of neural structures related to emotional behavior) process in an instant lead to a much more visceral sensing, an undeniable and almost indescribable *knowing*. This is the powerful feeling each of my parents experienced.

These two young dancers met that night, and four days later my father went out and bought a red convertible and an engagement ring. He picked my mom up for their date — with the top down on the convertible — drove her out to the beach, under a full Miami moon, and proposed to her. Clearly, my father knew how to make a great first impression. (They were married *one week* later.)

My parents shared this tender love story with my sisters and me when I was nineteen and taking my first nonverbal communication class. Their story inspired my many years of research into what I now call snap impressions, and a career of writing and speaking about the importance and power of these first takes in business and personal relationships.

I have been consulting and conducting research on nonverbal communication since 1982; my communication degrees emphasize nonverbal communication. I've taught the subject at the university level (*Time* magazine cited my Body Language course at Florida State University as one of the most popular college courses in the nation), spoken to government agencies and corporations, and coached everyone from executives and political candidates to people who want to improve their job-interview, sales, presentation, or dating skills. I've worked with judges, law enforcement officers, doctors, nurses, teachers, and foster parents. Nearly every week, I'm asked to appear in print and on broadcast media to comment on current events — from trials and scandals to political campaigns and celebrity behavior.

In this book, I use my expertise, including my academic background, continued research, and real-world experience, not only to give you the insights of science but also to show you how to put it all to practical, everyday use. I've also included stories that serve as examples of what I describe; many may strike a familiar chord. You will also have the opportunity to link to videos, online exercises, and recent research. As you read through these chapters, through the research and descriptions, think about the last meeting you attended, your most recent experience of meeting a new colleague or date, the telephone or email exchange you had yesterday, and all the other times when impressions mattered. As you recall these experiences, you will gain a deeper understanding of the concepts and learn more quickly how to interpret and use your nonverbal skills to your advantage. You'll learn to

- give the first impression that you intend to give, in a variety of circumstances;
- build your likability, credibility, and charisma;
- understand how power or the lack of it is communicated;
- read people quickly and effectively;
- understand that you are constantly forming "first impressions," even with people you already know as you begin a new interaction with them;
- discover how to get that rare second chance at a first impression;
- make a good "tech impression" with today's tech devices in today's many technological venues;
- recognize who you can really trust and how to be credible yourself;

- understand other people's actual agendas quickly;
- learn to trust your more accurate snap impressions and use them to guide you; and
- be more confident in yourself and your ability to interact with others.

The goal is to help you be — and be seen as — your best possible self while you also learn to quickly recognize and understand all the people you encounter. The result will be a more confident, courageous, and savvy you. Let's get started.

1. GETTING AND GIVING SNAP IMPRESSIONS

Use Body Language to Accurately Read Others and Improve the Impression You Make

Dana, a story consultant in Hollywood, had an appointment to meet with George Clooney. She'd had to postpone their meeting twice. "Unbelievable, I know," she said, laughing. "Who delays meeting George Clooney? But I had just had a baby."

The rescheduled meeting day arrived and Dana, exhausted by a sleepless night, threw on the only clothes that fit: white T-shirt, jeans, and a jacket. She hugged her new baby good-bye and then dashed across LA. As she was about to step through the studio's doors, a woman said, "Excuse me but do you realize your jacket is covered in spit-up?"

Dana, a true professional with a great spirit, whipped off her jacket and strode through the door to meet George. "I was so tired, and my baby was my priority. I really didn't have it in me to be nervous or play a part. I was just me — which that day included eau de spit-up."

In a snap, George loved her. She got the job, and George enjoyed her so much that for the run of their project, they always ended their weekly meetings with a one-on-one basketball game behind his office. Years later, Clooney told Dana what a unique first impression she'd made. "You were so real," he said. "There was no Hollywood fawning, just two people connecting."

I tell this story because, as we talk about the value of snap impressions, I don't want your awareness of the nonverbal cues you give and receive to make you overly self-conscious. It's most important to be present in the moment, connected, and authentic. The knowledge you'll gain here will help you do this so that the real you shines at its best.

How often do we hear someone say, "When I first met him, I thought…," "From the moment I met him, I knew…," or "She did not fool me for a minute…," or something similar? The first-impression process takes a few seconds or less. In fact, the most current research says that we can form an accurate first impression in 100 milliseconds — less than the time it takes to snap our fingers.[1]

We can process thousands of cues — whether visual, auditory, or tactile — and other nonverbal factors very quickly, so a snap impression occurs well before we've talked at length or exchanged business cards or email addresses. We form snap impressions not just when we meet face-to-face but also when we see someone in a photo, glance at her Facebook profile, read a text she has sent you, or hear her voice on the phone. We do this by noticing things we don't even know we are noticing, and most research shows that only long experience with someone can alter our initial hit.

Research done by Janine Willis and Alexander Todorov at Princeton University found that people make judgments about attractiveness, likability, trustworthiness, competence, and aggressiveness after looking at people's faces for just a tenth of a second. The researchers found that there was no significant change between snap decisions formed in one-tenth of a second and those formed during a longer exposure to a person's face. Given more time (up to a full second), people's fundamental judgment about the faces did not change. In fact, people became more confident in their judgment as the exposure time grew longer.[2]

The Science behind the Snap

Many regions of the brain are involved in forming and acting on a first impression. Research using fMRI (functional magnetic resonance imaging) on subjects as they formed first impressions of photographed faces and written profiles — each of which implied a different personality type — showed significant activity in two regions of the brain: the amygdala and the posterior cingulate cortex, or PCC.

The amygdala is a small, almond-shaped structure in the brain's medial temporal lobe. It is primarily responsible for processing emotional responses (such as fear and anxiety) and for storing memories of emotional events. But it also plays a role in interpreting body language and facial expressions, particularly when they may indicate a threat. It's the amygdala that helps you decide, "Can I trust this person not to hurt me?"

The PCC is involved in attention, memory, motivation, and decision making. It has been intensively studied in the field of neuroeconomics (which looks at brain activity and economic decision making) because of the role it plays in assessing risk and evaluating expected rewards or outcomes. Some researchers define it as hub connecting other parts of the brain. Both the amygdala and the PCC are interconnected with the thalamus.

The thalamus is *not* a limbic structure but it is involved in motor function and sensory perception. It functions as a relay station for two types of nerve impulses: those that carry sensory information (sights, sounds, tastes, smells), and those that control muscle movements. After receiving these incoming signals, the thalamus sends them to the appropriate part of the brain for further processing.[3]

(Go to www.snapfirstimpressions.com for two of my videos explaining more about first impressions: *How We Form First Impressions* and *Four Ways We Act on Our First Impressions*. Also, look for the link to the article "Recent Research on How First Impressions Are Formed.")

In a snap, everything you see, hear, and observe is quickly processed by your brain and mixed into the unique package known as a first impression. You look at someone for the first time and snap! Your brain takes a "photograph," taking in myriad cues all at once and forming a holistic image. These snap impressions use, in part, the emotional centers of the brain for this processing, and that helps to give them their powerful and lasting effect.

You may wonder, "How accurate can a snap be?" People are, on average, better than you might think at assessing certain aspects of personality and ability. A meta-analysis of forty-four studies measuring the accuracy of people's first impressions showed their impressions to be highly accurate.[4]

What You Say Is Not That Important

David and his roommate, Mark, were waiting at the bar for Mark's girlfriend. Looking up from his drink, David saw Mark's girlfriend come in with another woman — a black-haired beauty worthy of a *Sports Illustrated* cover shoot. Stunned by this woman's looks, David fretted over what he would say to make a good impression. He needn't have worried; nonverbal cues matter more than words in a snap. The warm looks David and the black-haired beauty exchanged in that moment led to a marriage that has lasted thirty years (so far)!

When it comes to first impressions, nonverbal cues pack more than four times the punch of verbal ones. When we are face-to-face with someone, we can see his expressions, the look in his eyes, where his head is placed, the way he is sitting, his physical distance from objects and other people, and the signals in his gestures, as well as perceive the warmth or coolness in his voice. Facial cues rank first among all forms of communication in their influence on initial impressions.

In a person's eyes we see interest, arousal, and power or sub-missiveness. In her gestures and posture we can understand her attitudes, level of confidence and optimism, and what type of relationship she might want. The amount of space she uses and keeps between herself and others helps us assess how much privacy she wants and how close emotionally she wants to be. We listen to a person's words to ascertain mood, personality, and honesty; we watch her hands and her touch movements to see how supportive and warm she is.

Nonverbal snap cues are so accurate — 76 percent accurate, or higher — for two reasons.[5] First, there is a genetic link between appearance and personality. We may have evolved to show our personalities on our faces and bodies because being readable makes it easier for people to socialize and interact, which is essential for survival. Just as the venomous Gila monster developed bright coloring over time that acts as a signal — the coloring tells potential predators that the lizard is dangerous — we have evolved to possess readability to make us appear *less* dangerous.

Second, our facial and bodily expressions reflect our emotions and, consequently, our personalities, and over time they become lasting facial features and body postures. We form snap impressions using body language and other nonverbal cues subconsciously and automatically, so they are not subject to unreliable conscious prejudices.

> One great use of words is to hide our thoughts.
>
> — Voltaire

Processing nonverbal communication is not an exercise in linear thinking. Most of the time, we, like David after he met the dark-haired beauty, cannot trace the steps we use to process the myriad cues available to us. Rather, the cues explode around us like fireworks, or they are like floats and balloons at a Macy's Thanksgiving Day Parade swirling before our eyes, or for many of us they just seem to come as feelings in the gut. For this reason, we may wonder if the conclusion we've come to is accurate. We may discount it, saying, "Oh, it's only a hunch." In reality, our hunches can be amazingly accurate.

Phillip Goldberg, in his book *The Intuitive Edge*, says that intuition "is the product of the mind's capacity to do many things at once without our being aware of them."[6] In a snap, we can, in less than forty seconds of communication, process up to ten thousand units of nonverbal information. That's ten thousand cues communicated between two people in less than a minute. We process that information into something valuable: an intuitive perception of the other person. The sheer volume of cues available to us helps make our first impressions reliable.

Think about it. If we totally disregarded the nonverbal cues, we would have only a few words, or perhaps sentences, in those first moments on which to base our impression. I don't know about you, but the words "Hello, my name is Joe" don't tell me a lot. Then consider how quickly and accurately we use nonverbal cues. In 1992, the researchers Nalini Ambady and Robert Rosenthal found that looking at short examples of behavior (examples lasting under thirty seconds) can lead to predictions as accurate as those based on observing behavior for up to five minutes.[7] Snap impressions are remarkably telling.

Forming a gut-level first impression is the first step in communicating. That impression dictates the reaction we expect to get, how we will relate to the other person, and all the other factors that affect how we form a relationship.

Right about now you may be saying, "I never make assumptions based on first impressions. I'm more sophisticated or more fair than that. I know better than to judge on mere appearances." Let me clarify. I'm *not* talking about reducing people to stereotypes based on prejudice or bigotry. I'm talking about the accuracy of your first gut-level reactions. There is a big difference. Gut-level impressions based on nonverbal cues are instinctual; prejudice and bigotry stem from learned cultural and social factors. They are part of our second-stage impressions. True gut-level first impressions are not subject to inaccuracy like stereotypes.

Stereotypes, in fact, undermine accuracy. For instance, one dramatic aspect of this process is the way we create self-fulfilling prophecies. We assign someone specific personality traits in the first few minutes, and then, as we interact, we collect information that makes our predictions about that person seem true, ignoring information that might contradict our stereotypical impression.

For example, a business owner interviewing contractors for a big job might see a candidate with a sweaty forehead and no smile, dressed in a gray T-shirt, coming toward him and think, "I don't want to hire this unprofessional guy to do this work." The business owner might not notice, however, that the contractor carries a clipboard, leans forward and nods as he listens, takes copious notes about what the business owner wants, and spends a longer time in the meeting than other potential contractors who bid for the job. All these latter cues are signs that the contractor is, in fact, being professional.

In the coming pages, we'll look more at factors that undermine our accuracy.

EXERCISE

Explore Your Snaps

1. Think of a recent instance when you met someone and formed either a negative or a positive snap of him or her. What did this person's body do? What was his or her voice like? Did the person's actions match his or her words? Record or recall

everything you can remember about your first few moments together and how you immediately felt in this person's presence.

2. Think of a time when someone formed an inaccurate first impression of you that you found out about. Perhaps it was a date who later said that he thought differently of you after spending more time with you, or a colleague who was initially biased against your joining his work group. Think back and try to recall your nonverbal behaviors at the first meeting. Were you nervous? Quiet? Tired? Stressed or insecure about anything? See if you can figure out what the other person saw when he saw you.

3. Ask yourself, "What are my three best qualities?" How do you express these qualities nonverbally? When people first meet you, do they recognize that you possess these qualities?

Survival Instincts

Cavemen and cavewomen knew all about first impressions. Out hunting for food, they were vulnerable to attack by strangers. If one of our caveman ancestors suddenly spied a stranger from an unfamiliar tribe, he had to make a very quick assessment — "Does he look like he will kill me?" Yes, we can trace the ability to form accurate first impressions to our primeval origins, when we needed to protect ourselves from potentially dangerous strangers. Forming quick first impressions is one of our basic survival instincts. When our ancestor saw that stranger from an unfamiliar tribe, he had to decide quickly how to approach him or whether to approach him at all, on the strength of a first impression. In a case like this, if someone's impression was not accurate, he — and his genes — would not survive. We are genetically predisposed to form quick, accurate first impressions.

In modern day-to-day situations, first impressions play a critical but poorly understood role. We still need to protect ourselves, and we still fear the unknown. When we meet someone, we need to know both whether it is safe to approach and how to approach and interact. We don't know his temperament or opinions. In a sense, we don't know if he "bites." So we assess him quickly. We may start by putting him in a category — safe or unsafe — and acting accordingly. This is vitally important for our comfort in a peopled world. If we could not do this, it would be too scary to leave the house, our cozy cave, at all.

If someone comes into work harrumphing and rolling her eyes, stands in front of you with her arms crossed and mouth twisted, and growls, "Good morning," you immediately form a first impression. For one thing, you know it's not going to be a good morning as long as you have to deal with this unhappy person. If people at a social event are standing in a circle talking to one another, and one of them smiles as you approach and steps aside to let you in, she is indicating that you are welcome and accepted. No words are exchanged, but you understand immediately.

> ## Stay Tuned In to Your Gut Instincts
>
> The first time you communicate with someone, pay attention to your gut. Do you feel safe interacting with that person? Have you ever called a friend, heard his hello, and known something was wrong? Did you change your behavior on the basis of that gut instinct? Whenever you begin interactions with people you know, check in at the gut level. What are they communicating on this day, at this moment? Do you need to step away, talk another time, or find out what's going on and give them comfort?

We may take for granted our understanding of these kinds of interactions, but if our gut-level impressions are to be useful, we have to pay attention to them.

Many years ago, I walked into a drugstore near my house

and saw a tall man with a mustache wearing a well-tailored, three-piece suit and holding a thin, unlit cigar as he stood nonchalantly near the magazine racks by the entrance to the store. I froze in place, and every fiber of my being screamed out, "Danger, danger! Leave the store now!" There was something about him I didn't trust. But I ignored that first impression. "This is a well-dressed man," I thought. "You're being ridiculous." So I walked past him into the store and did my shopping. When I went up to the front counter with my items, the well-dressed man was in front of me checking out. I looked at him and my whole body seized up and sent the message "Danger! Leave now." Again I ignored it, but I thought of something I had forgotten to pick up, and left the counter to go to the rear of the store. When I returned, the man was gone and the cashier stood pale and frozen behind the counter. I reached out and touched her arm, and said, "Honey, what's wrong?" She answered, "That man just robbed me at gunpoint."

Research proves that, while we need to create categories to understand our world, we must be careful of stereotypes, such as "well-dressed men can be trusted." As I mentioned earlier, stereotypes are maladaptive forms of categories. They do not correspond to what is actually present in the environment. In my case, the fact that he was well dressed had no bearing on whether or not he was a gun-wielding robber.

The moral of the story? Go with your gut. Even though I am an expert in body language, I ignored my first gut-level intuition of danger because it seemed illogical. However, my subconscious mind was busy picking up on little nonverbal details that told me the guy in the suit was not harmless. My limbic brain was processing cues, including the fact that a man in a suit, in the middle of a workday, was lingering by a magazine rack but not actually looking at the periodicals.

"This is weird!" said my brain, leading to my "Danger!" stress response. Later, at the checkout counter, though my conscious mind wanted me to ignore it, my limbic brain got me to leave that part of the store. I've had many instances of reading people with eerie accuracy at a first meeting; perhaps you have, as well. This story is a reminder to pay attention to the powerful intelligence processed with amazing speed in your deep limbic system.

In the movie *The Girl with the Dragon Tattoo*, the character Mikael Blomkvist, a journalist, goes to a suspected serial killer's house while his suspect is gone and finds evidence that the person is indeed a killer. When Blomkvist hears that person return to the house, he starts to run away. The killer politely asks him to come back into the house for a drink, and as the killer keeps making that request, we see Blomkvist standing with his feet and lower torso turned away from the killer, signaling his desire to keep on running. Blomkvist, ignoring what his body so clearly wants to do, turns around and goes toward the killer, even as we in the audience yell out, "No, don't do it!" When Blomkvist reenters the house, the killer greets him, revealing a gun and saying, "Our desire to be polite overrides our bodies' desire to flee danger."

In snap impressions, pay attention to your body. It can read clues about danger and then alert your conscious mind. Your body also signals other types of first impressions. In the next few days, as you meet new people, check in with yourself from your toes to the top of your head and see how you feel in the presence of each new person. Notice whether your body feels ill at ease or stressed in any way.

(Go to www.snapfirstimpressions.com for "Body Check In" — my instructions and a video on how to pay closer attention to your body's signals when you meet other people.)

The Gift of Intuition

Shortly after my drugstore incident, I read Gavin de Becker's bestseller *The Gift of Fear*. His premise: We are all "expert at predicting violent behavior. Like every creature, you can know when you are in the presence of danger. You have the gift of a brilliant internal guardian that stands ready to warn you of hazards and guide you through risky situations." We downplay this remarkable inherent ability. Intuition, de Becker writes, "is often described as emotional, unreasonable, or inexplicable." In general, "we much prefer logic." We "worship logic, even when it's wrong, and deny intuition, even when it's right."[8]

At his website — Gavindebecker.com — you can access information about signs we shouldn't ignore. Three important danger signals that he describes are particularly helpful to note when strangers make insistent attempts at conversation, refuse to take no for an answer, and press unwanted offers of help on you: these people seem to be charged up rather than discouraged by your tension, stress, or rejection of them; don't let you finish a sentence; or give you excessive compliments, touch you, and continue to touch you even when you freeze, block, or pull away. These behaviors may seem romantic in movies, but they are not comfortable in real life. A member of one of my first-impressions workshops came up after the break and told me, "I just realized my ex-husband gave all the verbal and nonverbal signals you showed us the day I met him. I was scared of him in that first meeting, but he was so overwhelming that I let him into my life."

(More insights into recognizing danger and understanding our stress responses can be found at my website, www.snapfirstimpressions.com.)

First Impressions Are Sticky

Not only do we form first impressions very quickly, but also, as research has shown, it can take up to six months of constant interaction to change an incorrect first impression. This means that if you meet someone who for some reason doesn't like you, it might take that person six months to change his mind and realize you're a wonderful human being. That's the power of the "primacy effect." We tend to assign more weight to our first impression than to our later impressions. The primacy effect means that first impressions affect all future thoughts about the person. They are resistant to change partly because they are connected to our basic survival instincts.

If we get good vibes from someone we meet, we may create what I call a "halo" around her. After that meeting, every time she smiles at us, makes full eye contact, or turns her heart toward us, we subconsciously note it and take it as further evidence of her niceness. Once the halo effect has taken hold, we tend to downplay any negative nonverbals we may pick up. If our friend is rude to a waiter, raising her voice and pointing her finger, we're apt to brush it off with "Well, the waiter was ignoring us." The halo makes it hard for us to change our first impression.

> ### The Power of Negative Impressions
>
> Dan met Donna, the wife of his friend Jay. "She was sour-faced and didn't look at me when I introduced myself," he says. "She left the room sighing and came back and dropped the baskets of chips and crackers in front of us and sat far away. That was ten years ago, and every time I am with her I see how far away she sits from me and how she rarely laughs, and I think, 'What a cold person.'"

The halo effect can be a marvelous thing. Research on happy marriages has shown that a spouse who fell in love at first sight may maintain a halo around his mate that allows him to be more forgiving of small transgressions. Noticing his wife commit a minor indiscretion, he is able to think, "Oh, well, that's a little blip on this incredibly marvelous person." This ability makes for a healthy, happy marriage. But as you might guess, the halo effect is dangerous if you don't notice a big ole blimp flying over you with flashing lights saying, "Danger! Danger!"

Negative first impressions stick as a result of what I call the "devil effect." Let's say that, on the morning of your first day on a new job, you are in the parking lot waiting to pull into a space that someone is vacating. Though your signal is blinking to show your intention to take the space, another car swoops in and steals it. The parking-space poacher hops out of her car, smiles and laughs, and then shrugs her shoulders, turning quickly and walking away.

Minutes later in your new office, this same woman stands in front of you and the other new employees and introduces herself as one of your new managers. Would you be impressed by her beautiful smile, confident gestures, and high-energy presentation? No way! In your first encounter with her, your gut said, "Inconsiderate and selfish." In your future interactions with her, you would find yourself looking for information to back up this snap.

Angels and Devils

Have you experienced the halo or devil effect? Take a moment to think about a time when you had a good first impression of someone, and about the information you gathered to confirm that impression. Were you rewarded with a good friendship or business interaction? Now remember a time when you had a bad feeling about someone and later learned your impression was correct. What specific behaviors did you see or hear that confirmed your impressions? How did you *feel* when you first met each of these people? How did you feel around them in later interactions?

(Go to www.snapfirst impressions.com for the video *Angel or Devil: First Impression*.)

The Bad Day Blues

Because of my work, I have been in airports and on planes almost every week for years. I have always observed that the world is full of kind and openhearted people. I've been a real Pollyanna.

But recently I fell off a small cliff and shattered my wrist. Shortly after surgery, wearing a bright blue cast, I traveled a distance to give a speech. In the airport security line, a guy behind me was pushing plastic bins around. One of those bins held my jacket, which fell to the floor. I had to struggle to pick it up with one hand — and received no help from Pushy Guy.

When I got on the airport train that carried passengers to the gates where we would board our flights, a teenage girl stared at me blankly. She refused to move so that I could get to a seat, and so, as the train moved, I fell to the floor. From there I looked up at the teenager's father. He said, "You should have held on to a post!" I was stunned.

This Pollyanna continued to find inconsiderate people that day — on the escalator and on the flight. I wondered, "Are people just getting ruder? What is the world coming to?" In fact, my impressions were colored by what neuroscientist Daniel Amen calls "emotional shading."[9] When your deep limbic system shifts into overdrive, you perceive neutral events through a negative filter. My starting from a bad place (I was in pain and worried about traveling with a cast) colored my impressions. All of us experience this, whether we are on the instigating or receiving end.

Is Your Mood Creating Bad Impressions?

Each time you get a negative first impression of someone, stop for a moment and reflect. If he seems rude or angry, cold or disconnected, ask yourself whether your mood that day is affecting your impression. Then take action to change your mood and theirs!

What You Can Learn to Change an Impression and Read Others

An enormous amount of research goes into nonverbal cues, and the studies can be fascinating. But how we act upon first impressions isn't just theoretical; it's wisdom you can — and should — put to use every day. Consider:

- You want to create affinity with a new customer or manager, so as you sit across the table from her, you smile as you begin talking. What else can you do nonverbally to ensure a good outcome? You will learn in chapter 5 how to use head nods differently with women versus men and torso leans to show you are interested.

- You are speaking to a small cluster of seated people and notice that one person has one foot pointed toward you and one foot pointed away from you, one guy just moved his feet apart, another's feet are crossed at the ankle, and both of your feet just turned toward the exit. What's going on? What do they think of you? Do they like you? You will learn that feet are the most honest portion of the body, and how they can show whether someone feels relaxed or nervous (see page 142); when someone wants to go (see page 44); that a person is signaling interest in you (see page 228); and even that someone is attempting to deceive you (see page 38).

- You see someone you are attracted to and keep glancing his way. What else can you do to encourage him to approach you, or to make it easier for you to approach him? You will learn about open-window-approach cues in chapter 2 and luring cues in chapter 4.

- A vendor says she can deliver the product on time and under budget. She raises her eyebrows and shows the palms of her hands as she speaks, and she says one of her words with a lilt in her voice. Can you believe what she's saying? You will learn about eyebrow flashes, honest palms, and vocal cues signaling honesty in chapters 2 and 3.

- A prospective client gives you a bone-crushing handshake. What can you know about him from this? What does he think about you? You will learn in chapter 3 the secrets to handling a bone crusher and why you might feel sorry for someone who wants to crush your hand.

- Someone asks you a difficult question. You pause and then answer in a voice two octaves higher than normal. How does that affect your credibility? In chapter 2, you will learn cues to avoid giving to others if you want to be credible.

- You've had a bad morning. As you face your day and meet new people or even see, for the first time that day, people you already know, how do you guard against being influenced by your less-than-rose-colored glasses? In chapter 1 and throughout the book, you will learn about moods that affect our first impressions, and how to change your mood and the impressions you make on others.

—⚍—

We've seen that snap impressions are quick, accurate assessments of others, and that they give powerful impressions to others. In the next chapter we'll explore exactly how these lightning-quick ideas are formed — and the four most important factors that form them.

2. WHAT HAPPENS IN A SNAP

Understand the Four First-Impression Factors: Credibility, Likability, Attractiveness, and Power

Marie was nervous about a meeting with a high-level executive, Ron, at his country club. Ron raised his eyebrows and smiled from across the room, approached, and said, "Marie?" When she nodded "yes," he tilted his head briefly and his smile grew and he continued walking toward her, with his hand outstretched, as though they were long-lost friends at a reunion, rather than a freelancer and potential client at an interview. Her tension about the meeting eased. Ron spoke warmly to Maria, as well as to the dining room hostess as she walked them to a table. He gave a friendly open greeting to their server and, once Marie was settled in her seat, turned his heart toward her and thanked her for coming to meet him. Though there were many distractions, he fully focused on her. "I like his confidence," thought Marie. "I thought I would be scared, but I'm not."

Marie very much wanted the work Ron might offer her, and felt a bit out of her comfort zone before meeting him. Yet almost instantly, she relaxed and felt comfortable, even safe.

—⊶—

Melissa thought she had found the perfect business part-ner when she met Jason. He was confident, attractive, and a great storyteller. He laughed all the time. When she first met him, and in later interactions, she felt "overwhelmed" by his enthusiasm and wit, but she would say to herself, "That's because I'm an introvert."

She noticed that sometimes there would be a swift change in Jason's demeanor. When a meeting was over and the other people had left, he would put on his lopsided grin and say something sarcastic about them. This would make Melissa uncomfortable, but again she would reason away her doubts, saying, "That's his sense of humor, and the clients love him." Jason was so charismatic that charm oozed out of him like honey. The problem was that the honey was so thick that Melissa couldn't see through it. Jason was a compulsive liar and a smooth talker, and he took her top clients from her, leaving her business in the lurch.

Something in Ron's demeanor immediately put Marie at ease. There was something about Jason's demeanor that charmed Melissa but also made her feel "overwhelmed" and "uncom-fortable." We know that we make snap judgments within sec-onds of meeting someone for the first time. But *what* is it that we see that can either put us at ease or set us on edge?

We assess four "first-impression factors" when we first meet somebody:

1. **Credibility:** This most important factor makes us feel safe because it tells us the other person is trustworthy.
2. **Likability:** This is what indicates that someone is warm, friendly, and easy to be around.
3. **Attractiveness:** Balance and symmetry in the body and face help create a positive snap for reasons that may sur-prise you. Other aspects of the power of attractiveness

inform your impressions and actions. But rest assured, it is not all about being pretty or handsome.

4. **Power:** Levels of dominance, either pronounced or subtle, exist in all our interactions and, ideally, send messages of confidence and ease in situations.

To understand how people use nonverbal behavior to make snap impressions, you need to understand these four crucial, primary factors. When you learn to recognize them, you will be aware of how they affect your perceptions of others, and you can form more accurate first impressions. You will also understand the specific things you can do at any time with any person to increase your credibility, likability, attractiveness, and power. I will also discuss how you can gain positive charisma, the extreme charisma exhibited by people who have high levels of likability, attractiveness, and power; what you can do to increase your positive charisma; and how you can be swayed more easily, and even fooled in ways that are dangerous, by highly charismatic people.

Credibility

As a first-time manager, Janet often sought the advice of Barb, a more experienced manager of another department in the company. The first time she met Barb, she felt at ease. And each time Janet sought Barb's counsel, she felt that comfort. It didn't matter if she came in upset with an employee or confused about a client's needs, when she talked to Barb she trusted her. Janet knew that if Barb said, "You did the right thing," she really meant it. There was no reason to worry that Barb would share her confidences with anyone else in the company, that she would say to someone, "You won't believe the crazy thing Janet said to a client."

At the same time, if Barb had a hard truth to tell Janet

about something she'd done wrong or could have done bet-
ter, Barb wouldn't hesitate but would tell it to her straight.
Barb's voice, face, and words would be earnest, and Janet
would never feel judged. Whatever problem she experienced,
she felt better for having shared it with Barb.

The most important factor in assessing others is credibility. Do
you feel at ease in their presence? Are they themselves and fully
present and attentive? When a person has credibility, she is who
she says she is, with no facade. You can trust her. In fact, the
words *credit* and *credibility* have the same root — *credo*, which
means, "I trust or believe." When someone is authentic, you
recognize this in both her facial expressions and her actions.
It really comes down to evolution: we are hardwired to pick up
on credibility. In forming a first impression, the basic survival
instinct says, "Can I trust this person? Can I feel safe in his presence? Is he going to pull out a knife? No, I can believe that what
I'm seeing is the real thing."

Before I teach the four factors of a first impression, I survey the audience, asking, "What is the first thing you notice
when you meet somebody?" Remarkably, in thousands of surveys, of audience after audience, year after year, I get the same
answers. People either specify credibility or list trustworthiness, authenticity, honesty, or integrity — all of which make up
credibility.

Your True North

Have you ever met someone who made you immediately feel
safe and at ease in his presence? Do you know someone you can
absolutely trust? The exercise "True North: Recognizing Credibility," which appears later in this chapter, will help you recognize credibility. In my programs, when audiences complete

the exercise and talk about their "True North people," who are credible, their voices grow warm — whether they are describing their mothers, new neighbors, CEOs, high school teachers, best friends, or new bosses. I listen and watch their nonverbal behavior as they pause with wonder and their bodies unfold. Their breathing deepens, moving from high in the chests to the bellies. If they are excited, they are also at ease and in general seem calm. And they always smile. They are reexperiencing what it feels like to be with a credible person.

One of the most important insights about credibility is that, when you are with someone who has it, you feel it in your body. Under stress our limbic system creates the freeze-flight-fight-or-faint response, but when we are in the presence of a True North person we feel the opposite of stressed. We feel not only safe but fully alive. And when you give others a True North impression, you feel comfortable and fully alive. Your body loves authenticity. If you try too hard to be someone you aren't, it exhausts you. If you are not behaving with integrity when you meet someone, even a short conversation can drain the life out of you.

Some people think it takes time to discover whether a person is credible. Time can certainly allow someone to build trust. But when a person behaves as his authentic self, as exactly who he is, no facade, you immediately develop a visceral feeling about him in his presence. And there's something else interesting about this: a credible person is credible to *everybody*. Other people see him the same way you do. Credibility is consistent and universal.[1]

When I first met John, he was a senior vice president of marketing at BMG, the entertainment conglomerate. I was struck by his credibility, and over the years this first impression proved accurate. He would take a call from the head of Disney's movie division, talk to an intern who came into his office, take a call from an überfamous musician, take a call from his boss, and turn to me, his friend, and use the same upbeat, happy voice. He is consistently himself with everyone; he gives each person his full attention while interacting with him or her; his gestures, the corners of his mouth, his voice, and his posture go "up" with enthusiasm; and the palms of his hands open wide as he talks, whether he is with his son, a musical star, or the waiter in a restaurant. He makes everyone instantly feel good. He is never "on" for important people and "off" while talking to others.

There are three classic components of credibility: competence, trustworthiness, and dynamism.[2] You'll find David K. Berlo and James B. Lemert's three components in the stories about first impressions that I've discussed so far:

- Competence is obvious in the knowledge and expertise expressed by the manager Barbara in her communications.
- Trustworthiness is evident in the sense of ease and safety engendered by the high-level executive Ron, in the honesty and sincerity of Barb, and in the warmth that John at BMG conveys to everyone he meets.
- Dynamism — a person's energy and confidence — is clear in John's consistent nonverbal behavior (which includes his energetic voice, his body language that moves and stays "up," and his open heart and palm windows) with everyone he talks to or meets.

You don't typically meet someone and say, "Hi, I'm credible." Rather, *nonverbal* communication — your facial expression, the quality of your attention, your expression of welcoming openness — is vital in demonstrating competence, trustworthiness, and dynamism in a first impression.

Seven Ways to Lose Credibility

I am often asked to determine the credibility of people in the media. For the History Channel special *The Secrets of Body Language*, which airs periodically, I was asked to focus on some famous — or infamous — moments in recent history. Here are some examples from that special and from other classic loss-of-credibility moments (specific cues that hint people may be lying) that I have analyzed and that show the power of nonverbal cues to change, in a snap, the impression a person gives. You can do things that make people doubt the veracity of a particular comment you are making and affect your snap only in that moment, or you might have a more lasting impact.

- A sports star is asked if he has used performance-enhancing steroids. He pulls his feet under the chair, and each time he replies, he gives a fluttered blink and the left side of his face lifts up in a smirk.

- In a historical State of the Union address, the president smirks twenty times, so that the two sides of his face are mismatched. He makes tongue thrusts (brief movements of the tongue out of the mouth) more than fifty times as he talks about education and health care, and even at

The Eyes Have It

The most noticeable nonverbal behavior affecting credibility is eye contact. Studies find that maintaining a steady gaze while communicating promotes credibility — especially the speaker's trustworthiness and competence — and that avoiding eye contact undermines credibility.

You may recall that former vice president Dick Cheney accidentally shot his friend Harry Wittington while on a quail shoot. In a televised interview four days after the incident, the vice president consistently looked down and to the right while making his main statement about the incident. For many observers, his credibility plummeted when he did so. It further eroded when he spent his interview time talking about his pain, calling the day one of the worst of *his* life, instead of recognizing it as likely one of the worst days ever for his injured friend.

the end of the speech, when he says, "the United States of America."

- In a 2011 interview, everything Charlie Sheen said was overridden by the effect of his glazed eyes, disheveled hair and clothing, and manic gestures. And, guess what: he smirked — a lot.

- In the White House press conference during which Bill Clinton said, "I did not have sexual relations with that woman, Monica Lewinsky," he touched his nose approximately every four minutes. He also paused oddly, in relation to his normal speech pattern, and he gestured out of sync with his words, using a finger that was crooked, not straight.

- When Oprah Winfrey asked Jay Leno about his feelings toward Conan O'Brien, he said, "I have no hard feelings at all." But as he said this, Leno frowned, moved an arm across the center of his body, shielding his heart, and rubbed his ear.

- A judge in a well-known reality competition show rolled his eyes, smirked, and told one contestant, "You were great," while looking away. (Okay, maybe that made him an interesting judge to watch.)

- A presidential candidate said, "I love the United States of America and all it stands for," while shaking his head "No" several times. Later he said, "I love America" and shook his head "No" again.

(For more examples, go to www.snapfirstimpressions.com and view the videos *Ways You Can Lose Credibility in a SNAP* and *Are They Lying?* You'll see in a snap how people display nonverbal behaviors that affect their credibility in negative ways. And you'll see how even seemingly small behaviors can affect a person's credibility.)

EXERCISE

True North: Recognizing Credibility

1. Think about someone you trusted straight off the bat, or after interacting for only a short time. If no one springs to mind, consider a person you have known for a long time whom you trust, or even a public figure you consider trustworthy. This is your "True-North person." What is it about this person that makes you feel this way? How does this person behave? What does he or she say that makes you trust him or her? How do this person's facial expressions, posture, or hands, or the rest of his or her body, transmit integrity?

2. Imagine your True-North person in your mind's eye. Write down details about his or her demeanor and nonverbal behavior. If you recall your first meeting with this person, describe it in as much detail as you can.

3. Imagine yourself in the presence of your True-North person. Reach back and remember *how* he or she made you feel. How did you feel physically? Did this person make you feel heard, seen, and understood? How did this person initiate a conversation? How did he or she stand or sit? How could you tell that this person listened to, focused on, or was generally interested in you? Is there something about this person that you want to model? Is there something in his or her behavior that reminds you of yourself?

   Understanding why this person is your True North increases your ability to recognize this kind of person elsewhere — and to be this kind of person to others. Once you're able to recognize a

> True-North person, you can calibrate within seconds whether someone or some situation "feels good" or "is not right."

Seek Models of True North

Vistage International is an organization that helps leaders within companies, and owners of companies, become more successful. Once a month, small-business owners and high-level executives meet in groups with one another and with an adviser from Vistage, who chairs the meetings. Each chair interviews and selects his or her group members, facilitates the meetings, and coaches each member one-on-one. For many years, I've given talks to Vistage groups on credibility and deception detection, and I am fascinated by the credibility shown by Vistage chairs. They possess many behaviors that I admire and seek to emulate.

For example, when Ben, one these chairs, called to prep me for my meeting with his group, I felt he really wanted to talk to me and wasn't simply rushing through a to-do on his list. The use of time as part of communication, called "chronemics," can create a powerful snap. Ben was happy to spend time talking to me, and this increased his likability. As he talked about each member of his group, the tone of his voice and his speaking rate matched what he was saying. As I discussed earlier, a match between a person's nonverbal behavior and the words being said creates credibility and makes us feel safe and comfortable as listeners. Ben sounded sincere when he mentioned that he liked something about a member of the group; when he shared something a member could improve on, he sounded caring.

At the meeting, I noticed that Ben spoke to everyone the same way. Each member of the group relaxed and opened up as Ben talked. With all the high-status people in the room, there could have been tension and competition, but Ben's authentic presence put everyone at ease. After the meeting, he took the time to pull two seats over to a corner of the room and sit down with members individually. I talked to a member later who said, "This group is full of people who own companies and have to appear perfect to the world, but here we trust Ben so much. We know he sees us as strong people, and yet we feel safe enough to tell him anything — and cry like babies if we need to."

Credibility and Synchronicity

When an honest and credible person speaks, her body language, facial expressions, and paralanguage are all synchronous with the words being spoken. (*Paralanguage* refers to vocal features that are nonverbal yet still contribute to communication, such as pitch, volume, intonation, and tempo. All these can be used to subtly modify meaning or convey emotion.) You can detect deception by watching for a lack of synchronicity between any of these elements. When a person's spoken words don't agree with her accompanying nonverbal communications, we should give the nonverbals more weight.

As in the examples of Sheen, Clinton, and Leno mentioned earlier, words (which are conscious) can be used to deceive, whereas

What Credibility Sounds Like

Paralanguage, or vocalics, refers to all the nuances of the voice except for speech. Just as *paranormal* defines behavior that is outside the normal, *paralanguage* defines meaning given outside of words — the volume, pitch (high or low), rate of speech, and its quality. Prosodics, a subgenus of paralanguage, includes intonation, stress, vocal emphasis, and rhythm.

Paralanguage is *how* words are uttered. This can include whether they are *spoken* unusually fast and loud, as well as unusual "um" and "ah" pauses; coughing and throat clearing; and a tense, higher-than-normal voice. Notice the vocal utterances that occur in the first moments of an interaction. You will be surprised to find that they are windows to the person, that they reveal how honest and open that person is going to be with you.[3]

body language (which is subconscious) is much harder to control and use in this way. For example, when interviewed, people who answer either negatively or affirmatively should have congruent head movement. It's common for those who are lying when they say, "I did not do it!" to nod their heads up and down in a contradictory nonverbal yes as they speak. People may also shake their heads no while saying yes. For example, the wife of presidential candidate Herman Cain shook her head almost violently no while saying, "He respects women."

What's Wrong with This Picture?

In one of his first interviews after the largest oil spill in history, Tony Hayward, British Petroleum's CEO, wore neat, pressed vacation attire. He spoke about the spill in a relaxed manner and smiled as he did. He brushed off any talk of friction between BP and the Obama administration: "The extent of the cooperation that is taking place, I think, will be seen as a textbook example of how to do an emergency response."

Many viewers were struck by a disconnect between the circumstances and Hayward's words and demeanor. Stock phrases like *textbook example* downplay the seriousness of a situation and connote insincerity. A credible person shows nonverbal behavior that matches the circumstances. Hayward could have demonstrated credible care, concern, and understanding had he worn work clothes and work boots, allowed emotion to animate his voice, and used words emphasizing that there was nothing routine or textbook about the spill's impact on the human and wildlife populations affected. Hayward was soon forced to resign his position, at least in part because of the snap impressions he gave viewers in his communications.

To form our impression of a person, we compare what we think would be normal or appropriate words and nonverbals with the words and nonverbals we hear and see. Hayward's words and nonverbals did not match what many felt should be expressed by a person leading a company responsible for a horrible crisis.

Credibility Cues

Nonverbal communication is the way the subconscious mind speaks. No matter how much you want to control it, your nonverbal behavior gives clues about how you are truly feeling. We can base our interpretation of these clues on a number of factors called deception cues. They help us spot liars and recognize what in our own nonverbal communication establishes credibility.

When someone is telling the truth, she *feels* the truth in her emotional brain (limbic system). She responds to this feeling with nonverbal behaviors. Then the neocortex, which is responsible for words, is activated. An honest and credible person feels, shows, and then speaks in ways that match; the brain moves from feeling, to showing, to speaking. What you want "leaks out." If you want to ensure that you give an impression of credibility, the first thing you should do is think about your underlying motivation in the situation. Whether you're a salesperson, teacher, parent, or manager, what you really want comes out. Do you want to manipulate someone, or do you want to help? Do you want to appear trustworthy and sympathetic, or just look that way while someone is watching?

"Feel, show, say." When someone is being honest, he might sound more melodic and his movements, voice, and words will seem to flow smoothly. Someone who is lying thinks about the information he wants to hide. He thinks of the words he wants to say in the lie, and he may say the words super quickly before he forgets them. He has to think about how to transmit what he should be feeling, which results in awkward, oddly timed verbal and nonverbal messages. You have heard, seen, and felt it when someone says, "It is a pleasure to meet you," but takes a long pause before actually looking at you and smiling, and then lets the smile linger too long. When you listen to or watch someone lie, this lack of synchronicity between the verbal and nonverbal messages alerts the central nervous system and creates a stress response. You can see how important it is to get an accurate impression of someone you're listening to, and being in the presence of someone who is lying is stressful.

When someone feels guilty or fears being caught in a lie, he might freeze in place like a teenager caught by his parents in the part of his story he didn't rehearse. He might wear the famous frozen, deer-in-the-headlights look that Tiger Woods exhibited at the beginning of his apology statement. Freezing gives us time to decide what to do next. The liar might flee, so he may give nonverbal signals of leave-taking by pointing his feet toward the door, tucking his feet under a chair, or pointing his lower body away from the person or people he is with. He might place his feet far apart in what I call the "lock-and-load" position, or place his hand or hands on his hip(s). These moves make him appear bigger and more threatening, and they signal that a person is ready for a fight. Or he might suddenly lose the color in his face as the blood rushes away from the surface of the skin, leaving him looking like he might pass out at any moment.

Lies that are planned in advance can sound credible, but

A Person's Stress May Be Visible in a Snap

A stressed-out person may do one of the following:

Freeze: Freeze in place for a moment.

Flight: Move or position all or parts of her body to flee, or try to make her body smaller to create a smaller area for attack.

Fight: Position her body to fight by getting bigger, placing her feet farther apart, moving her arms up, or putting her elbows out.

Faint: The blood can flow away from the surface of the skin.

there's apt to be "nonverbal leakage." Liars expend so much effort trying to remember the lies they made up that they give out more cues, from eyeblinks to foot pointing, called "leakage," than do spontaneous liars.

> ## The Lock-and-Load Power Position
>
> Notice whenever anyone makes you lock and load your stance, planting your legs far apart, or if anyone locks and loads as you talk to them.

In order to most clearly read deceit, you need to know the person's normal baseline behavior. This might be tough to recognize if you are reading someone you just met, but there are tools that make it easier. For example, notice whether the speaker is pausing. Some people talk fast and loud, and some people talk slowly with lots of pauses. Liars tend to go to the extremes of their normal behavior patterns with regard to expressiveness and pausing. Extroverts tend to be more expressive when lying — raising their voices, laughing, cracking jokes, changing the subject, or getting in fights. Strong emotions such as humor and laughter provide great cover behaviors to hide liars' nervousness. Introverts, on the other hand, become more introverted. They might freeze up, slow down, get quieter, make less eye contact, or become wooden, giving their voices less vocal variation. As you might guess, this means we are more likely to recognize when introverts are lying. It is easier for extroverts to charm us into thinking they are telling the truth when they cover their lies by being more bombastic.

The Timing Is Telling

A sports star accused of wrongdoing holds a press conference to deny the charges. He clears his throat and begins speaking; it's a simple case of nervousness, perhaps. But listen closely as he continues to speak. Is his throat clearing a baseline behavior, or does he do it only when he makes certain statements? Notice the timing. Does his voice go up in pitch, and does he clear his throat or cough after he says, "I am innocent"? And does he clear his throat again after bringing his voice down almost to a whisper and saying, "I did nothing wrong"?

Feel It First

Depending on how you define the term *muscle*, there are about six hundred to eight hundred muscles in the human body. It's impossible to consciously manage or control them all. What's more, if you do work to control your body's language, your subconscious will simultaneously continue to send its own messages.

Remember, when someone is being honest, she feels something first, then shows and says what she feels. A deceiver, especially if she has time to prepare her deception, is thinking of her story and the words she needs to say. But there are so many muscles in the face that you can't control all of them when you're under stress. It's difficult for a person to avoid sending a constant stream of signals about what she is really feeling and thinking.

If you try too hard to control your body, you'll likely send mixed messages. One part of you will say one thing, while another will say something else, and the result will be that people trust you less, not more.

Morgan is a petite, shapely blonde who doesn't lack for men coming up to her and flirting. Her complaint is that these encounters never end in the men requesting a date. She is highly successful in her business, but in social settings, she says, "I smile, laugh, and do all the things that should work, but they still end up walking away."

One evening, I go out with her, not as her wing woman, but as her barstool coach, to watch her interactions from a discreet distance, hidden from her view. I notice that the men are picking up on her tension. Morgan smiles and laughs, but her smile lingers longer than it should, and her laugh is a bit brittle and forced. She radiates tension. Even her shoulders and eyebrows are noticeably raised, as if she is afraid. Her voice is high and strident, and her hands occasionally rise up and push out, as if she is stopping traffic. She is pushing the guys away!

The men sense her fear, and I can even see some of them try to be less assertive by taking up less space and tilting their heads to put her at ease, but she is unwittingly making them uncomfortable. Morgan has a lot going for her, but it is undercut by the discomfort she evokes in others. When we talk, she is not surprised by my observations. "I wasn't doing any of these things simply because a body language expert was watching me. I have always felt nervous while flirting, and I just thought my bravado masked it!"

We addressed her fear, working "from the outside in," deciding what she could do differently. We worked on changing her stance and gestures, relaxing and lowering her voice and shoulders, and calming her tension. We even changed her breathing so she was able to breathe deep in her lower abdomen and feel more relaxed. She ended up getting dates, including a very special one with the man who is now her boyfriend.

Likability

Sharon and Scott opened their door to greet their friend Spencer and his new wife, Debbie. Debbie came in with shiny eyes, her arms up and open, and her head tilted, exposing her throat. Her palms were showing, and she greeted her hosts with a warm, melodious voice. Though Sharon had never met Debbie, her guest's greeting was so warm and gregarious that she won her over immediately. An hour later,

*after dinner, Sharon remarked to Debbie, "I feel like I've
known you for years!"*

When a person demonstrates likability, she smiles and laughs
easily and uses friendly upper-body language. She shows emotions and facial expressions that allow us to know how she's feeling. The opposite of likability is a lack of expression and affect,
and, often, a monotonous voice. Research shows that the more
expressive someone is, the more comfortable we are with her.

Why We Love Extroverts

Extroverts tend to give more positive first impressions.
Remember, when we can read someone's emotions easily we
are more comfortable around them — which puts introverts
at a disadvantage when it comes to creating a good first
impression. If you are a nice, quiet person who wonders
why slick players and high-maintenance drama queens get
all the attention, know that there is science behind this
love for "madness at first sight." Happy, healthy extroverts
seem confident and expressive, which are things we like.
Even extroverts who display red-flag warnings with their
over-the-top, supersized gestures still make a great first
impression. This expressiveness — at which the extrovert
excels — may aid the few dangerous extroverts in their
successful deception.

Introverts, on the other hand, who naturally pause to think
before they speak, who talk softly, display fewer gestures
and expressions, and make less eye contact, don't fare as
well on first blush. Introverts' ways may appear to be signs of
deception. We may wonder why they are so quiet, why they
stumble over their words and make so little eye contact, and
this may make us suspicious of them.[4] Understanding these
differences between introverts and extroverts can help you
read and interact with them more effectively.

A person who demonstrates likability does so in person,
online, and over the phone. You know it immediately. And, like

credibility, likability is universally recognized. We can recognize likability in the first split second when we meet someone.

Likability includes, but is not exclusively about, commonality. We like people who are like us, but likability is more about personality, warmth, and friendliness. People who are likable turn and look at you. Like Debbie when she met Scott and Sharon, they open their bodies to you when they speak. Likability welcomes connection.

Amy went to her fiftieth (yes, fiftieth) high school reunion and remet a high school pal, Rob. It was love at first re-sight. They said they knew they were reunited soul mates. To introduce him to her friends, Amy had a dinner party. Imagine this strange new guy meeting Amy's friends, many of whom had known her for thirty or more years and were highly protective of her.

Rob was at the door to meet Amy's friends as they arrived, hugging them warmly. Throughout the evening he spent time with each one, leaning in to talk and in one case touching his listener on the arm to emphasize his emotional point. He obviously worried less about himself than connecting with each person. If something were between him and another — such as a sofa pillow on the couch or a vase of flowers on the table — he gently and subtly moved it out of the way. Rob spent time with Amy, too, as the evening progressed, but he also gave each of her friends his rapt attention. As they shared stories, his face and body language fully reflected their emotions. He laughed with them and sighed with them. At one especially emotional point in the evening, when stories of a loved one lost to AIDS were shared, he cried with them. Of course Amy's friends all loved him.

What's to Like? — Cues That Make You Likable

Several characteristics contribute to likability.

Moving toward: We go toward what we like and move away from what we don't like. This is a foundation principle of body language, and it is related to our primal orienting reflex. Instinctually we move toward what we like, desire, or want, and move away from what we fear, distrust, or don't like. You can move toward someone by stepping nearer to him or by simply tilting your head, upper body, or whole body in his direction. Leaning your body toward another says, "I'd like to be closer to you." It also tests whether he will reply in kind. Think of how you pose for a photograph with another person or a group: everyone leans in. This is something we often do when we're listening intensely, which is another way to show our particular interest in someone.

What do you think is the most honest portion of the body? Think about the part of the body under the least amount of conscious control, and the part of the body that is often first to change in response to stress. Did you guess the feet? The feet point to where the heart wants to go. When we are stressed, our feet may freeze in place, point away to flee, plant themselves far apart so that we can fight, or go out from under us as we faint. We stand with both feet toward the door to signal that we want to leave a conversation, or, more politely, we place one foot toward the speaker and one toward the exit in a subtle, little "please let me go" plea when we want to wave good-bye.

Opening windows: We have what I call "body windows," which we seemingly open or close while interacting with others. Our feet, knees, pelvis, stomach, heart, neck, mouth, eyes, and palms are the body parts that act like open or closed windows, depending on how we orient them in relation to other people. Likable people tend to keep their windows open by orienting their body windows toward others, unfolding their limbs, and keeping barriers like desks, cups, drinking glasses, and purses from coming between them.

Reaching or pointing: Think of the trained hunting dogs who point their bodies toward prey so the hunter can find it. A person interested in you may subtly point at you with a foot or knee, cross his leg at the knee so his foot is facing toward you, reach a hand partway across the table, or point his face toward you. These are all signals that say, "I am focused on you."

Eye focus: In this electronic age, with so many distractions, it feels great when you have someone's full attention. They aren't looking around the room, distracted by others, or glancing down at electronic devices. They look and listen until you have finished speaking.

Facial and auditory feedback: Clear, readable facial expressions and lots of them — smiling, brow furrowed in concentration, slow nodding — and perhaps small sounds like *uh-huh* and *mmm* show interest. These are examples of warm and/or enthusiastic, expressive paralanguage.

Matching: Subconsciously, people demonstrate their comfort with the people they talk to. When you reflect the other person back to him, he feels affirmed and that you are aligned with him. If you lean forward, he leans forward. If you cross your legs, he will cross his. If you reach out across the table, a comfortable person will demonstrate likability by doing the same. While seated at a table, he will move glassware, papers, and other objects out of the way so that nothing distances him from you. Conversely, a person who is ill at ease or lying will place things between the two of you — a purse, a coffee cup, a cell phone, or some other object.

Touch: It's helpful to briefly touch the person you're speaking to. I know what you're thinking. "Are you crazy? I don't want a stranger to think I am weird, or to have a new coworker charge me with sexual harassment!" Yes, in our current culture we fear all kinds of touch in initial interactions, and even handshaking has decreased significantly. But touch is powerful, and it works because nonthreatening touch positively affects our chemistry. A brief, nonthreatening, nonsexual touch can change how we feel in less than a fortieth of a second.

Match and Mirror

To establish commonality nonverbally, match the body posture and facial expression of the person you are speaking to, as well as her energy level, gestures, tone of voice, and even rate of speech and breath. Do this unobtrusively while maintaining eye contact. When you match another person, an interesting thing happens: you actually begin to feel what she is feeling. In addition, you communicate at the subconscious level: "Hey, I get it; I'm with you," or "I want to understand you," or "I'm not your enemy."

Don't mirror aggression. If someone stands over you and yells, with feet planted broadly, legs apart, and hands on hips, don't jump up out of your chair and match this behavior. Instead, if it feels safe to do so, subtly come in at a level or two below her energy. Inject a little intensity into your voice as you say that you understand she's upset. Express your interest and concern. Then slowly bring your volume down, slow your rate of speech, and relax your body. Your would-be opponent will likely slow down — and calm down — with you.

Touch is an essential element in our development and health, and a powerful way of communicating.[5] I have been studying and conducting surveys on touch since my first graduate-school research paper on the subject, "Haptics (Touch) in Initial Interactions in Business Settings." I even did research on touch in initial interactions in my role as Canada's national spokesperson for Vaseline Intensive Care lotion. Over the years, I have discussed with audiences many fears and concerns related to touch, in programs on body language, gender differences, and sexual harassment. But touch offers so many benefits, which should motivate you to touch in safe, nonsexual ways. There have been many studies on how touch affects first impressions, and they show it has positive effects. For example, in one study, subjects who were asked to sign a petition were touched lightly on the arm when the request was made, and 81 percent complied. When the experiment was repeated with a different request, 70 percent of those touched complied; only 40 percent of the untouched individuals did so.[6] A restaurant server's fleeting touch on the customer's hand or shoulder results in larger tips. Of course there is a caveat: 8 percent of people in the United States don't want to be touched. (Go to www.snapfirst impressions.com to watch the video *Five Ways to Use a Safe Touch to Make a Positive Impression*.)

Attractiveness

Traveling to speak at a convention, I went to the airport straight from the gym. I was wearing my favorite old and stretched-out sweats. My hair was pulled back in a ponytail and, okay, a tad sweaty. Needless to say, there was no makeup in sight. No big deal, I figured; I didn't know my fellow flyers, and they didn't know me. We would never meet again.

Upon arrival, I waited with a large group of people for the bus that would take us to our hotel. I noticed that everyone waiting seemed to know one another, and that many had been on the flight with me. These sixty or so people were well-dressed (in suits) and well-coiffed. They also were giving me odd looks or averting their gaze. As we boarded, none of them offered me access to the empty seats next to them. As I made my way to an empty row in the back of the bus, I saw, on the laps of some of my fellow passengers, the convention brochure with my picture on it! These were the people I would be speaking to the next day — and I looked like I'd just gotten out of bed.

We live in a visually oriented culture in which our appearance not only precedes our words but can overpower them. Research shows that individuals tend to agree on their snaps of strangers even when these strangers vary in race, nationality, and culture, and even when their impressions are based solely on facial appearance.[7] But appearance is only one aspect of attractiveness, so before you plan on having plastic surgery, read on.

What Is Attractive?

This measurement has a lot to do with symmetry. Research shows that a person with body and facial symmetry is highly attractive. Cate Blanchett, Halle Berry, and Michelle Pfeiffer display bilateral facial symmetry. So did Elizabeth Taylor — a line from her obituary in the *New York Times* in 2011 reads, "As cameramen noted, her face was flawlessly symmetrical; she had no bad angle, and her eyes were of the deepest violet."[8] A *Newsweek* cover story, "The Biology of Beauty," specifically mentioned Denzel Washington as a star whose face had been measured and deemed to be perfectly symmetrical.[9] Bilateral symmetry — in which the body or face is perfectly balanced — has a subliminal effect on first impressions. When we say that a person's body or face is "perfectly balanced," we mean it can be divided into identical halves by drawing a line down the center; the right half will be a mirror image of the left half. Scientists believe symmetry is seen as an indicator of a person's freedom from disease and of worthiness for mating and reproduction. Other researchers hypothesize that a face or body that is bilaterally symmetrical is easier for us to read.

A lack of symmetry is uncomfortable for us to view; it can alert the central nervous system that there is something amiss. When I teach deception detection, I show what a lack of facial symmetry looks like: Simon Cowell's mouth twisted into a one-sided smirk as he judges a performer, or a twitch lowering one side of the mouth of a sports star as he says he never used steroids. When the right and left sides of the upper and lower halves of someone's face are asymmetrical, or the sides of the body are asymmetrical, as when, say, someone stands with one hand on her hip or leans to one side, we see the incongruence. It indicates that the person is confused or puzzled, doesn't understand something, is unhappy, or is in one of a long list of other uncomfortable states.

Between the Sexes

I am at my favorite restaurant, sitting outside with two of my girlfriends. Three slender girls in pretty summer dresses walk in and sit at the bar. Within twenty minutes, eight men, puffing up their chests, surround them and lean in to get closer. As my friends and I watch, the men compete to see who can pull out a credit card faster to pay for the girls' drinks. My friends and I smile, watching men in the pursuit of their idea of beauty as we order another round of mojitos, one dessert, and three forks.

There is a stronger consensus among men regarding which traits are attractive than there is among women, according to a study published by a Wake Forest University psychologist.[10] More than four thousand study participants rated photos of young people (age eighteen to twenty-five) for attractiveness, using a ten-point scale that ranged from "not at all attractive" to "very attractive." But before the participants rated the photos, members of the research team went through the photos and judged the essential characteristics of the people depicted in them — qualities like "seductive," "confident," "thin," "stylish," "sensitive," "well-groomed," "classy," and so on. Breaking out these factors helped the researchers determine which common characteristics appealed most to men and women.

Perhaps not surprisingly, the men's ratings of women's attractiveness centered primarily on physical characteristics. They rated most highly those women who were deemed to be "thin" and "seductive," although many men also favored "confident" women.

On the other hand, there was little consensus among the women as to which subjects were attractive. As a group, they tended to favor "muscular" men, but some women gave high attractiveness ratings to men that other women said were not attractive at all. Women seem to be programmed to find all sorts of men attractive, perhaps so that they do not all compete for the same Tarzan-like he-man. In fact, while most men have the same standard as other men when deciding what is attractive, women tend to be more individual, having a standard of attractiveness that is eerily similar to the man they are in a relationship with, or have recently been in a relationship with.

Women find men who look like their current boyfriend or current mate the most attractive, and, as they change love interests, they change what they find attractive.

The good news for women — and men — is that you can affect your attractiveness by feeling more confident. Most of the men in the Wake Forest University study rated women who looked confident as more attractive. My roommate in college had a great way of creating a likable, confident first impression. It sounds odd when described, but it worked. She would pause at the entrance as she walked into any room, her shoulders back, her chin slightly raised, her arms slightly extended, and her hands open, as if she were offering the room at

Attraction and the Halo Effect

Research shows that we believe what is beautiful is good. We favor facial symmetry and we like a balanced body silhouette. When we meet someone we find attractive, our snap impression of that person is generally much more positive than our snaps of those we find unattractive. Research shows that the positive and more lasting impressions created by attractive people affect how they are treated by teachers, juries, college admissions committees, managers, and job interviewers.

large a hug and waiting for the men to notice her and come into her arms. They did.

Most of us would claim not to be so shallow as to judge people on their looks, but research indicates that we do judge others in that way. For example, an attractive boss is liked more and generally perceived more positively than an unattractive boss. In an online survey of 61,647 people (a very large subject pool) by *Elle* magazine and MSNBC in 2007, "good-looking bosses were found to be more competent, collaborative and better delegators than their less attractive counterparts."[11] This is another example of the halo effect. When we see outstanding positive characteristics in individuals, we assign them other positive qualities as well.

And in a 2008 study at Tufts University in Medford, Maine, psychologists Nicholas Rule and Nalini Ambady asked students to rate faces according to their perceptions of the competence, dominance, likability, facial maturity, and trustworthiness of the faces' owners. The students did not know they were judging pictures of the CEOs of the highest- and lowest-ranked Fortune 1000 companies. The students' ratings of each CEO closely corresponded to the CEO's company's profits.[12]

What Can We Do about "Lookism"?

When the actual personality and character traits of individuals have been studied, stereotypes about attractiveness have proven false. Good looks don't make an individual particularly "good" in other ways.[13] Next time you get a warm, fuzzy feeling about someone you've just met, ask yourself if this is based on superficial good looks.

Still, we all want to feel good about how we look to others, and there are things we can do to boost our attractiveness quotient and improve the impression we create. Remember the disheveled me who was mortified to find herself surrounded by future audience members on the bus? In that moment, I couldn't change my appearance, but I could change how I felt about myself and how I behaved in order to help people feel more comfortable with the sweatshirted me.

I began to walk up and down the aisle of the bus, stopping to say hello and introducing myself. I joked that I could use a refresher course in the first-impressions training I'd later be giving all of them! Instead of cringing and cowering, I assumed an air of confidence. My comfort, my going toward rather than away from them, my warm laughter-filled voice and handshakes made it easier for people to look past my appearance and, I hoped, trust and like me more than they would have if I had schlepped to the back of the bus and hid (as my embarrassment would have otherwise led me to do). I was pleased to see the smiles as people leaned in to greet me warmly.

There may be times when you need to go "outside-in" and fake it till you make it. Keep in mind that, however you hold your body, it begins to chemically influence how you feel in as little as one-fortieth of a second. Briefly taking on confident, charismatic, likable behaviors until your body chemistry catches up makes you feel confident inside.

One of my clients who has participated in my body language programs had a brain tumor removed and is paralyzed on one side of his face. He has been struggling because people are not comfortable around him. I've been helping him in one-on-one coaching do things nonverbally to help people cope with his appearance and lack of facial symmetry.

We can all make simple, small changes in our body language, voices, and approach to others to improve our attractiveness. Remember that, while we find attractive people more likable, we also find likable people more attractive. So incorporate behaviors discussed in the "What's to Like?" section earlier in this chapter to create a more attractive snap impression.

Power

The speaker came onstage with shoulders back and chest high and moved to the front of the platform. He showed his confidence in his recommendations by using gestures that mimicked a conductor's baton coming down just as he made each important point. He also struck a beat with his open hand by pounding his fist into his palm. He paused to let his points sink in, and, in the silence, he looked out at the group, gazing deeply into people's eyes.

Another speaker came onstage with shoulders slumped and head bowed. He stood behind a table, bent over his laptop, his feet together and his hands glued to the keys of his computer. Occasionally, he glanced up at the screen behind him, where his slides were projected, and read his bullet points aloud. His ideas were well supported and his speech was well prepared. But his nonverbal delivery? Not powerful.

We've all experienced power in first impressions. We walk up to someone and shake hands, each of us noting whose grip is more forceful. When we make eye contact, we notice who breaks away first. Is one of us nervous and the other calm and confident? Beginning with our snap impressions, we're subconsciously deciding who is going to have more power in the interaction.

Power is communicated in numerous ways — the four foundational principles of power are confidence, space, openness, and relaxation. You demonstrate power through the amount of space you take up with your body, through your possessions (coffee cup, purse, computer tablet or pad, smartphone), through your voice, and through whether your body windows are open or closed and whether your body is tense and distracted

---

> ### Be the Queen of Your Jungle
>
> Imagine a lion in the jungle. She establishes her space and territory with relaxed confidence. She moves gracefully. Her posture is open as she stretches out her limbs. She'd never have to battle for an armrest on an airplane! She's authentic, fully herself. Without baring her teeth or making a threat, *she* is in charge.

or relaxed and focused. This isn't purely about being dominant. It's about assuming a confident stance, claiming and holding the space you're in, and being open (positioning your body and face toward others) rather than closed (fearful and self-protective).

In a study of 132 business school graduates that took place over eight years and included extensive interviews, researchers looked at women who show power by means of aggressiveness, assertiveness, and confidence — traits normally labeled as masculine. They discovered that women who can turn their power on and off according to their circumstances (called self-monitoring) get more promotions than either men or other women.[14]

How to Look and Feel Powerful and Confident in a First Impression

You can meet another's power with your own without coming to blows by making use of the following tips.

- Note how much space you take up in your walk, in your stance, and as you sit; you don't want to take up too much or too little space.
- Maintain eye contact. Trick: look from one of the other person's eyes to her other eye to the bridge of her nose, then back to each eye.
- Touch the other person, either before she touches you or immediately after.
- Be the first to extend your hand for a shake.
- If you're on the receiving end of a power shake, in which someone surrounds your handshaking hand with his

left hand, or is overly aggressive in his greeting, reach out and hold the other person's elbow with your free hand as you shake.

- If you are normally the quiet person who is interrupted frequently, and you're interrupted when you are not finished talking, continue to speak. Know that, if you are interrupted, it is okay to very slightly raise your voice and even raise your hand a bit with the palm facing toward the interrupter.

- Don't hide behind your "stuff." Don't put your belongings — coffee cup, electronic devices, and so on — between you and others. Similarly, if you are presenting and are offered a podium or table, stand in front of or to the side of it instead of behind it.

- Select a prominent seat — a noticeable position at the center of the conference table or in the front row of a large meeting. This signals confidence, genuine interest, and your willingness to engage.

- Show respect for hierarchies but don't be overly deferential. If your aim is to advance to the next level of your profession, strive to be a colleague rather than a subordinate. Visit the offices and cubicles of powerful people, ask them to lunch, spend time with them. Positive power is contagious.

- Notice how far apart your feet are in a normal stance. Now move your feet one inch farther apart to create lion-like stability and presence.

- Square your shoulders and let them relax to communicate strength and stability.

- When anxious, we often fidget or touch ourselves for reassurance. Minimize acts such as rubbing your earring or mustache, twisting your hands, pushing back your hair, and so on. Research indicates that powerful people do move — they might tap their feet or click their pens with impatience — but this is not behavior you want to model.

Some aspects of nonverbal communication that generate a power impression are permanently set. Of course you have heard that greater height and bulk give people more power, and research shows that people with deeper voices are also more apt to have power or be perceived as more believable, and more likely to have their requests carried out. If you don't have these physical attributes, work the bullet points in the preceding list especially hard!

I'm a short blonde woman. Early in my career, I was often told by my audiences that, when I was first introduced, but before I actually spoke, I didn't appear to be a credible information source. I found out that, even though they knew I was a credentialed expert, they were thinking, "What is this little blonde going to teach me?" I learned early to appear "bigger" by projecting my gestures outward and making my voice lower and louder.

Conversely, some very tall people need to soften their appearance. The power of height can be so overwhelming that others back down, back away, or just don't interact. Power isn't about intimidation.

> ### Observing or Participating?
>
> Your company culture might have powerful people who sit in the back row or even in chairs pulled behind the back row so that their backs are against the back wall. Oddly, these seem to be the seats where people of power sit, as part of cultural norms. Unfortunately, this position might indicate a lack of engagement and/or can make it appear as if they are there to critique or judge the proceedings. These are not the qualities of truly powerful people.

Charisma

Charisma comes from the Greek word *charis*, which means "grace." Research shows that people with charisma are able to gracefully persuade us to buy from them, vote for them, and mate with them. Charisma intoxicates and persuades us.

Charisma is based on three of the four first-impression factors — likability, attractiveness, and power. A person who has a high level of these three characteristics also has charisma. Charismatic people take up space, relax, maintain laser-focused eye contact, focus on their listeners completely so that the latter are the center of their attention, keep all their body windows open to others, energize their listeners, and smile all the time. Do you know someone like that?

Research says that when someone's charisma is high, it overrides our ability to tell whether that person has the fourth important first-impression factor: credibility. In other words, highly charismatic people have an easier time getting away with lying. Can you think of anyone in your life or in the public eye who has charisma but lacks integrity?

Not all highly charismatic people are dishonest, but be aware of and savvy about the potentially blinding effects of charisma. When you meet someone you find highly charismatic, pause, check up on his credibility, and remember to use your "True North" as a guide.

Charisma without credibility can be extremely powerful. In fact, sometimes it can be much more powerful and persuasive than what you hear or believe in. Watch a televised political debate with the sound off and see which candidate appeals to you. Or the next time you see a charismatic movie star in a long TV interview, turn the sound off and see what stands out. Researchers Daniel J. Benjamin, an assistant professor at Dartmouth and a fellow at the University of Michigan's Institute for Social Research, and Jesse M. Shapiro, of the University of Chicago, examined the effects of charisma on politics in a study using Harvard undergraduates. Two hundred and sixty-four students viewed soundless, ten-second video clips of unfamiliar candidates from fifty-eight past gubernatorial elections. They "were able to pick the winning candidate at a rate significantly better than chance. When the sound was turned on and participants could hear what the candidates were saying, they were no better than chance at predicting the winner."

The researchers found that they had to use silent clips to measure charisma because, as Benjamin said, "We found that snap decisions based on charisma are a good predictor of election outcomes. But you need to measure charisma with silent video clips rather than sound-on clips because knowing about candidate policy positions disrupts people's ability to judge the non-verbal cues that really matter."[15]

So, to determine whether someone has charisma, we may not need to hear that person speak. But do not be fooled by someone who is both charismatic and dishonest. How can you identify those who are both? You'll have to listen to and watch them much more closely. As I mentioned in my discussion about credibility, the timing and congruence of nonverbal behaviors with actual spoken words can reveal whether someone is lying. When someone is telling the truth, her entire body aligns with her words. In addition, credible speakers exhibit facial symmetry between the upper and lower halves of their faces when speaking. Look for this when considering your social, business, and political snaps — and when dealing with someone who is highly charismatic.

(Go to www.snapfirstimpressions.com to view the video *Charismatic People: The Good, the Bad, and the Both*.)

—⁓—

Next, let's explore how to interpret and convey the four snap impression factors — credibility, likability, attractiveness, and power — in our personal and professional lives.

3. MEET AND GREET

Get Off to a Great Start with Handshakes and Other Greetings

My friend Jerry has been a customer service trainer for more than a decade and repeatedly gets high ratings from his audiences. But early in his career, Jerry found that it took what seemed like an eternity to get the audience to warm up to him and give him their full attention.

One day, a fellow trainer invited Jerry to watch her teach a course. Jerry sat in the back of the room and observed as his more experienced colleague made sure to greet each person who entered her workshop. She shook each person's hand, introduced herself, asked for the person's name, and then repeated the name. She personally welcomed each person to the program.

When the workshop started, Jerry's colleague seemed to have immediate rapport with her participants. He vowed to try her "handshake technique" at his next presentation.

He did and the difference was astounding. By the time the workshop started, Jerry felt that he'd already made a personal connection with each person in the room and they with him. People started participating within fifteen minutes of the class starting, whereas it used to take at least a half hour to an hour to get them all involved and contributing to discussions. He could not believe the difference.

The average person shakes hands fifteen thousand times in a lifetime.[1] But the choices of where, when, and with whom to share a handshake, and whether to shake hands at all, have changed over the past few years as the business culture has grown more casual. We are also exposed more often to people who have different religion- and culture-based touch and greeting norms, and to members of the germaphobic Purell generation as they enter the workforce or step into leadership roles. Shaking hands remains an important ritual for us to understand, use with ease, and appreciate as a source of first-impression information. Recent studies indicate that a firm handshake — held with a complete grip — showing strength and vigor, along with eye contact of an appropriate length, creates a favorable first impression in North America. In fact, the handshake is the quickest, most effective way to establish rapport with another person.

Research in the United States also shows that it takes an average of three hours of continuous face-to-face interaction to develop the same level of rapport you get *instantly* with a handshake. Yes, a handshake is equal to three hours of interaction. It's amazing that you can shake hands with someone and, in that moment,

Instant Rapport with a Handshake

When I was in graduate school and read the study that concluded it takes an average of three hours of continuous face-to-face interaction to develop the same level of rapport you get instantly with a handshake, that fact stuck with me. Feedback from audiences at my talks and seminars has validated that finding many times, but I can no longer find the original research. It seems amazing and yet perfectly believable that a handshake can make someone feel as comfortable with you as talking with you for hours. Try it out yourself. Shake or don't shake, and see what happens.

make him feel as safe and comfortable with you as if you'd been talking for hours.

Handshakes Come First

So many of my clients and audience members have asked about handshakes that I have been conducting survey research on the topic for many years. Not surprisingly, my survey research shows that the handshake remains the generally preferred greeting for initial meetings by 84 percent of women and 98 percent of men.

Many cultures have greeting rituals — from handshakes to bows to *namastes*. They all create a stop position that puts greeters at a safe distance and gives each person a full view of the other's body from the feet to the top of the head. Basic handshake rules in North America: walk up to a person, stop approximately sixteen inches away, and shake hands. In business, we greet someone in this manner and then step back to stand a minimum of two and a half feet away to talk.

Often there is no other form of touch in the critical first four minutes of an interaction. If you don't shake hands, you miss out on so much. In my experience, many awkward first encounters that end with miscommunication occur because the parties did not have the safety check of a handshake. I'm not sure why this is true, but if you think back through your own encounters, you will likely find that those without handshakes did not go as well as those with handshakes. Shaking hands provides vital information and an opportunity to connect, so don't skip this important greeting.

When Do You Shake Hands?

This is one of the top questions asked by my audience members. The general guidelines for when to shake are as follows:

- When you are introduced
- When you say good-bye
- When an outsider visits you in your office or place of business
- When you seal a deal or finish signing a contract
- When you offer congratulations
- When you encounter someone you know from a business or social relationship outside the confines of your office
- When you first enter a business or social setting and greet people you already know
- When you exit any business meeting, especially those attended by outsiders
- When you want to signal that your interaction with a stranger has become more significant than it was when you first began. (If you've ever had a conversation with a stranger on an airplane, you probably didn't shake hands until you knew you wanted to talk further. Sometimes people won't shake hands until the end of the flight; they shake then to indicate that they enjoyed the conversation and would like to speak again.)
- When you want to show others in the room that you respect and accept a certain person, and to demonstrate that you regard that person as safe
- When you want to show another person that the space she is entering into, and the group she is joining, is safe.

There are many opportunities to shake hands, and each one offers a wealth of information.

The Body Language of Handshakes

We subconsciously read open, empty palms as indications that a person will be honest, open, and trustworthy. It is not surprising that religious leaders and religious figures throughout the ages have been depicted with open palms facing forward.

Biologically, the hands' temperature and the moisture of the hands, too, communicate important information. Hands get cold under stress. When we shake hands with someone whose hands are cold, our primal brain reacts with a danger response — "This person isn't calm; is that because he's nervous, afraid, or about to attack?" The palms of the hands sweat in response to stress; so if you have sweaty palms, this will signal to others that you are nervous and may be dangerous.[2]

Finally, you instantly exchange chemicals through the skin in a handshake, and this gives you a chemical read of the person whose hand you shake. These chemicals also provide a mnemonic device, a way for us to remember the person, if not his name, in the future. This is yet another good reason to shake hands. (The chemical read occurs in the more primitive part of the brain, which produces stronger memory links, while names are stored in the neocortex.)

Handshake History

In Western cultures, we shake hands to greet another person or to seal a contract or promise. Most historians believe that the handshake once demonstrated that neither party was about to use a weapon. In ancient Rome, men would put out their right hands in greeting because the right hand was the weapon-holding hand and the left hand shielded the heart. Each would grab the other's forearm and clasp it tightly so neither man could attack. Holding on to each other's forearm made it difficult for them to kill each other! Medieval knights made the shift from arm clasping to hand clasping and later to shaking. The shaking began when some knights started hiding weapons up their sleeves. The vertical shaking pattern was designed to cause any weapons hidden in sleeves to fall to the ground. The intent was clear: handshakes were weapons checks.

What's in It for You?

Have you ever walked into a meeting late and not had the opportunity to shake hands with the other participants? Or come to a social event after everyone else has greeted everyone and shaken hands, and you didn't have a chance to do so? Have you ever gone to shake someone's hand and had that person fail to reach out? How does it feel when you have to interact with someone in such circumstances? In written surveys that I've conducted with over two thousand subjects total, the number one response to the question "How do you feel (in any situation) when an offered handshake is not reciprocated?" is that the individual feels uncomfortable. The next-most-frequent responses are, in order, that the would-be handshaker feels left out, snubbed, or disconnected.

The handshake signals acceptance into the "tribe," and when given by one member it shows all others in the vicinity that you are to be accepted. If we don't get this acceptance, it's natural to feel awkward, uncomfortable, disconnected, or even snubbed. With a handshake, we and another person can reach rapport in seconds. Give yourself that opportunity.

A study on handshakes undertaken by the Income Center for Trade Shows demonstrated that people are twice as likely to remember you if you shake hands with them. The trade show organization's research also showed that people respond to those with whom they shake hands by being more open and friendly. Other research demonstrates that shaking hands makes you more likable. Shaking hands increases your ability to persuade others and increases the likelihood of a sale. My own research shows that my speaker friend Jerry was right: audiences listen more intently, are more polite, and give a higher credibility rating to a speaker if the speaker shakes hands with them or with a representative sample of the audience. In other words, it *pays* to shake hands!

A participant in my program took what I said to heart. She worked at her company's corporate headquarters and started standing near the door at the Friday meetings and shaking hands with everyone, introducing herself to those she didn't know as they came in the door. Three months later she was promoted to a dream job she hadn't even applied for. She learned through the grapevine that, when the job opened up, the executives said she would be perfect. They said she was confident and got along with everyone. She took the job and got a $10,000-a-year raise.

Manshakes

Though men have been shaking hands for thousands of years, women only began shaking hands on an equal basis with men in the 1980s. Men in American culture have long had what I refer to as a "secret handshake." Up until recently, the secret was to pump the hand up and down two to five times.

Why so many pumps? As with many other male species, modern North American human males participate in a dance of power when meeting. They use the handshake to size each other up. This takes time and proximity, hence the numerous handshake pumps. They look for nonverbal signs to see who will be the alpha male — whether one will control the interaction — or if they are meeting as equals.

However, in the 1980s and '90s, men in cutting-edge or laid-back cultures such as California began shaking hands with only one pump — anything more branded you an out-of-towner. That style has now become the norm. Except in a few metropolitan cities, very formal interactions, and international business meetings, the one-pump handshake is the new secret handshake.

No Great Shakes

A well-known author went to speak to an audience of students working toward their MBAs. She shook hands with some of the students before the speech. During her speech, she went to

Rules of the Game

Every year I go around the country speaking to court reporters. Court reporters are the people, predominantly women, who record every word said in the courtroom or in a deposition. They have a lot of stories about the lawyers they work with.

Many of them talk about a particular handshake ritual they see at the beginning and end of a trial or deposition. Male lawyers who have known each other for years come in and shake hands with each other. Then those same lawyers spend the entire day or trial saying what might seem to outsiders to be horrible, derogatory things about each other, shaking their fists and rolling their eyes. They, in effect, go to battle with each other. But when the deposition or trial is over, they get up, walk over to each other, smile, shake hands again, and say, "Let's go out for a drink." They are buddies again.

The court reporters tell me they are flummoxed. How can you shake hands and be friends again with someone who treated you so abominably?

What they are seeing is men using the rituals of gamesmanship. The game rules say, "Shake hands with your opponent and come out fighting." When the game is over, the game is really over, so you leave your bad feelings on the playing field and shake hands again. This ritual is repeated by men over and over on playing fields as they grow up, so in adulthood it's second nature to them to shake hands and come out fighting. Only in the past couple of decades has the research shown that there are women who now understand the principle of gamesmanship. Who are those women? The ones who frequently played coed team sports when they were girls.[3] Whether you're a woman or a man, if you don't use the rules of gamesmanship and shake hands at the beginning and end of interactions, you might lose your chance for a fresh start or second chance at a first impression next time.

shake hands with a student in the audience who was about to participate in an exercise with her. The student wrinkled up her nose, puckered her mouth in disgust, turned away, and said, "I don't shake hands." The author was stunned. She froze in place with her hand out. The student was not embarrassed by this, but instead merely added, "You have germs."

The author later told me, "In an instant, this affected that student's reputation in my eyes, and my impression of the rest of the students and the institution as well. Normally, I happily offer advice and mentorship to anyone in my audience. This time I didn't."

Human resources executives and small-business owners that I consult with say they now have people come in for interviews who refuse to shake hands. Clients whose companies stand among the Fortune 500 have asked me to train their employees under age thirty-five in basic greeting etiquette. They report an increase of people in this age group refusing to shake, or feeling uncomfortable when shaking, hands with coworkers during the workday. They even encounter new salespeople who say they won't shake hands with prospective clients or customers.

Even though a handshake confers enormous advantages, some people prefer not to shake hands. The number one reason listed is a fear of germs. Young people under twenty-five are especially fearful. Research conducted in 1997 by Market Facts of Chicago revealed that 51 percent of Americans wish they could wash their hands after shaking another person's hand. Their survey also indicates that women are more concerned about germs than men are. While 57 percent of women wish they could wash their hands, only 44 percent of men have the same concern (these figures were rounded up).

It's interesting that this change occurred after 1997, when Purell hand sanitizer was introduced as a consumer product. (Purell sales lead the rapidly growing market for alcohol-based disinfectant gels, which currently is valued at $90 million annually.) That year was also when, after I had spent years speaking about first impressions, my college audiences became the first to ask me how they could *avoid* shaking hands.

Reality check: You can get germs from shaking hands, and sanitizers can reduce the amount of certain types of bacteria on the hands. But many things we touch all day long — door handles, water faucets, the buttons on elevators, the keys on the copy machines — hold germs. A memo passed around the office holds germs for up to twelve hours! However, you're not going to form a close personal relationship with a door handle. At least, I hope not. Go ahead and shake hands; it can help you establish that you recognize you are with a human being — and wash or disinfect afterward if you must.

(If you would like more information about handshakes, including my prediction about the demise of the handshake, go to www.snapfirstimpressions.com.)

Secrets of the Perfect Handshake

Few things can create an effective first impression as clearly as a gracious, easily given handshake. But unless your father took you aside and gave you tips as a teenager, most likely no one told you the ideal way to shake hands. Based on my research, here is the best way — in North American culture — to engage in the perfect handshake:

Rise, if seated. That rule used to apply to men only, but now women too should rise. If you remain seated when someone is introduced to you, the personal indifference you communicate is unmistakable. The only approved exception to rising to shake hands is when you are eating. And in that case, you not only can wait to rise but can also wait to shake hands until after you are done.

Approach the other person with confidence. Keep your head level and your hands at your side.

Keep your hands free. Be sure to keep your hands out of your pockets, since research indicates that we don't trust people with hands in their pockets. Make sure your right hand is free to shake hands. Always shift any object you may be carrying — a purse, briefcase, papers, beverage, or cell phone or other electronic device — to your left hand before you begin the greeting. Ideally, keep electronic devices out of view for the entire interaction.

Smile briefly. Don't overdo it. If you smile too long or too much, you can be perceived as submissive. An overextended smile can create a negative impression, inadvertently pegging you as over eager, easily manipulated, or unintelligent. Women need to take special care not to overextend the smile, as it can reduce personal power and even be misinterpreted as a sexual come-on.

Make eye contact. Good eye contact increases feelings of trust. Don't stare, but don't look at your shoes, either. Making eye contact as you approach lets the person know you want to interact. Men need to extend the eye contact for at least three seconds without blinking or looking away as they shake hands. Women need to be careful about holding eye contact for more than three to five seconds at a time with men they have not met before. Research shows men may perceive extended eye contact with a woman they have not met as a sexual advance.

Face the person heart-to-heart. When you stand at an angle instead of facing the person squarely, you send the symbolic message that you are not being straight and open. You may look as if you need to protect yourself, you do not like the other person, or you feel the need to reduce the intimacy or the duration of the interaction.

Make sure your hands are clean and dry. If you have a problem with clammy hands, wipe them on your handkerchief or a tissue before you shake hands. At social functions, carry any iced drinks in your left hand, so your right will not be cold and damp when a handshake is called for.

Strike out with your right hand and arm across your body to your left. The forcefulness and confidence of the move lets the other person know you not only want to shake hands but also look forward to it.

Make sure your whole arm reaches out. An arm held closely to the body indicates timidity and lack of confidence.

Offer your hand with the thumb on top. The thumb on top is symbolic — it indicates you want equality in your interaction. No one person will dominate. You will respect the other person and expect him or her to respect you.

As you stretch out your arm, open your hand between the thumb and the first finger. This ensures that you can slide your hand easily into the web of the other person's hand. Make sure the rest of your fingers are together, and your palm flat rather than cupped, so palm can touch palm. Tilt your fingers down and scoop your hand upward into the other person's hand to avoid getting just the ends of their fingers and ending up with a wimpy handshake.

Make palm-to-palm contact. Open palms symbolically show a desire to be open and honest in your interactions; a closed palm communicates a lack openness and honesty.

Once full contact is made, wrap your fingers around the other person's hand. The pressure should be equal to or at the most slightly greater than the pressure the other person applies. Never grip the other's hand in a contest of macho handshaking to see who can hold on the hardest or longest. You want to have a firm handshake, but the rule is to match the pressure or add to it only slightly.

Firm It Up

Men often tell me that their fathers taught them to shake hands. Inevitably, they say their dads emphasized having a good strong grip. A firm handshake is important. Research shows that a firm handshake indicates positively your extroversion and emotional expressiveness. The majority of people do not want to do business with someone who offers only a wimpy handshake. Research also shows that men tend to have firmer handshakes than women do, and that people see men and women with firm handshakes as more extroverted, "open to experience," and less neurotic and shy.[4]

Cultural Differences

Not all handshakers think you should have a firm handshake. In certain parts of the world, including India, some parts of Malaysia, some parts of Africa, and some Muslim cultures, the rule is to give a *soft* handshake to show respect and demonstrate that you have no intention to harm the other. A firm handshake would indicate you don't trust him. Can you imagine the misunderstandings that could arise?

A pharmaceutical sales rep for a new medication for epilepsy knew that doctors are hesitant to recommend or change patients' epilepsy medications for fear of triggering seizures. He knew that he had to sell to the thought leaders in this field, and his challenge was to persuade these knowledgeable people to look at the research on his company's medication. He realized that three of the thought leaders were originally from India, and he had heard that, in India, you give a soft handshake to show respect. He consciously changed his handshake, and not one or two but all three immediately told him, in effect, "You are the only sales rep who shows respect."

These doctors were now willing to look at the research and recommend the medication to their peers. That year the sales rep won the salesman-of-the-year award for his company. He said in his acceptance speech that he had found a reverence for recognizing cultural differences.

Palm-to-Palm Contact Is Key

In researching the topic of handshakes over many years, I have discovered that even more important than the firmness of the grip is the contact of the palms. We want to make full palm-to-palm contact because, when you are reading body language, you observe the palms of the hands to discover if someone is being honest with you and is willing to self-disclose. If someone shakes hands with you and gives you just her fingers and not her full palm, at a subconscious level you may think, "What is she hiding? What is she keeping from me?" It doesn't feel right.

Similarly, I have discovered that many women arch the palms of their hands when they shake, precluding palm-to-palm contact. They give various reasons for this, such as shyness, lack of confidence in themselves or in their handshakes, or, most often, not wanting men to think they are forward or giving a sexual signal. Granted, palm-to-palm contact can be construed as intimate, but it is that way for a reason. It symbolically says, "I will be open with you." In fact, men say they dislike it when women arch their hands, and they characterize such women as stuck-up or cold.

The most important finding in my survey research is that people, especially men, do not want to interact with someone who gives them a wimpy handshake and would even prefer to interact with someone who gives them a bone-crusher handshake. At least with a bone crusher, you know what you're getting! After a wimpy handshake, men and women surveyed felt they hadn't received enough information about their partner.

How to Read Handshakes
and Respond Appropriately to a Bad One

You've probably experienced many of the following types of handshakes in various social and business encounters. Now, you'll better understand what they mean and how to form (or not form) a good working relationship with the person. Now, for every encounter, you'll have a quick indication of the person before you actually begin the meeting.

Ouch! The Bone Crusher

Have you ever had someone give you a bone-crusher handshake? You wanted to squeeze back, maybe even wanted to make him suffer, but you couldn't because your hand was locked in a vise grip.

Why people give bone crushers: People give bone-crusher handshakes for a variety of reasons. One reason is simple cluelessness: they have no idea that their handshake is painful. Another is habit. Typically a handshake style becomes ingrained and is practiced over many years. Perhaps the bone crusher is offered by someone who remembers that first practice with Dad and the desire to impress him. The snap impression of a bone crusher is often "This person has a big ego." But the real reason for most such handshakes may surprise you. I have found that over 80 percent of people who grip too hard actually have low self-esteem. Fear and insecurity motivate them to start out overstrong. Or they have low self-esteem that they compensate for by offering handshakes that make them look confident.

How to deal with a bone crusher: When you are dealing with a big ego, you are usually better off letting him crush away and have his thrill. If you really need to start the interaction on an equal footing, so that you each have equal power, use the following technique. When someone grips your hand too hard, your crushed hand is helpless to respond, but your other hand is totally free and available. So take that free hand and wrap it around the offending hand. This sends the message "Hey, you're surrounded. Lighten up." Interestingly, I have found that crushers will not register what you have done on a conscious level, but on a subconscious level they know you are a force to be reckoned with.

Women can consider taking their free hand and gently patting the offending hand, sending the message "Bad boy" or "Bad girl." Almost magically, the crusher will ease up on the vise-like grip. However, if you are a man shaking hands with another man, I do not recommend the patting gesture.

As far as your handshake is concerned, bear in mind that your strength of character is not directly proportional to the strength of your handshake. You don't need to break small bones in order to prove that you're a powerful, straightforward, upstanding person.

The Two-Handed Handshake

What it means: The two-handed technique lets you know at a subconscious level that the other person views himself as a force to be reckoned with, and it may also serve other purposes. Depending on the amount of pressure, location, and manner in which the person positions his outside hand, he can send many different messages. For example, gently resting the left hand underneath the handshake symbolically says, "I'm here to support you." You may have gotten this kind of handshake from your doctor or religious leader. Gently placing the left hand on the outside of your hand while smiling warmly at you can communicate warmth and extend friendliness. This is something you see mainly in the southern United States. However, exerting heavy pressure changes the dynamic into a two-handed vise grip, and this may make you feel not only surrounded but overwhelmed or controlled. The location of the left hand can send another message if it moves up your arm into what is called "a politician's handshake." The farther up the arm, the more the person is exerting control and trying to control you physically and symbolically.

What you can do: As the person grips your right hand (and possibly arm) in both of his hands, you may choose to place your left hand on top of the handshake to show that you will not be overwhelmed. Top-down pressure usually communicates the desire to be Alpha, but in this case it shows your desire to be equals.

Up and Down

What it means: A hand offered with the palm down shows that that person's power is important to him, and that he wants to come out of your interaction "on top." When someone offers his hand to you this way, you may think you are left with no option; if you want to meet his palm, you have to place your hand on the bottom as you shake his.

What you can do: However, you are not stuck on the bottom. Here is a subtle trick: As he approaches with his palm down, you can take his hand and shift your weight forward on your right foot, as you normally would when shaking someone's hand. At the moment you shift your weight, gently and quickly turn your palm halfway over as it meets the other palm, so both of you end the turn with your thumbs on top in an equal handshake. You don't need to turn your hand all the way and put the other person's hand on the bottom. He would notice such a shift consciously, just as he would notice it if you tried to pull a Bruce Lee and flip him! Instead, just bring both hands to an equal, upright position.

If someone puts out his hand with the palm up, it shows that he wants to support you and may go along with your ideas. This is the handshake I most often see offered by ministers, doctors, nurses, counselors, and others who want to show their desire to support you.

The Never-Ending Shake

"So I walked in to meet him, and he wouldn't let go of my hand. Even when we stopped shaking, he just held on. It felt awful!" Ever hear someone say this? Or maybe it's happened to you? The ritual of the handshake is so specific, we could even count in seconds how long it should last. When someone does not let go, it feels bad.

What it means: In man-to-man handshakes, there is an undercurrent of competition when one holds the other hand captive. There's a great scene in the remake of the movie *Ocean's 11* in which a character destroys a car salesman's confidence simply by holding his hand in a lingering captive handshake.

Competitiveness can also be the case in male-to-female handshakes. However, many women report feeling that the man who does not let go of a woman's hand in a handshake is really giving her a sexual come-on. Sometimes women even feel violated by a lingering captive handshake.

What you can do: So how do you get out of it? Well, the natural response would be to pull away with your hand and to lean or step back. But that just makes the other person hold on tighter. In addition, by pulling away you show fear and weakness. Instead, follow the "Let Go, Ego" rules:

1. Shift your weight forward over your right foot (the foot your weight naturally rests on while handshaking). Don't lift your foot. Just gently shift your weight forward so that your upper body is in the other person's intimate space. You are now in the space we usually reserve for attacking others. It's a subtle attack, brief but potent, just long enough to discombobulate the other person. Don't bow, bend at the waist, or step forward.

Bowing or bending makes you look weak, and stepping forward draws too much attention to your movement.

2. At the same time that you shift your weight, splay your fingers and break downward. Because you have put the other person off center in the same moment with your shift, he will have momentarily loosened his grip enough for you to break out of it.

3. Shift your weight back again. If you linger in the attack zone, the other person will know what you have done, and you will signal your intention to remain aggressive.

What Else You Can Learn from a Handshake

Sometimes, a person doesn't have to do more than touch your palm for you to make a snap impression. Here are things you can discern with that first skin-to-skin touch of palms.

Clammy Hands

Have you ever shaken someone's hand and found it was so clammy that you wanted to dry your hand afterward? We do not like wet handshakes. We associate sweaty hands with fear. When we shake someone's sweaty palm, we may wonder what that person is afraid of, or what he is hiding. (The hands are the only parts of the body that perspire solely in response to stress. The rest of the body perspires from stress as well, but also in response to temperature.)

Dry hands indicate that you are socially secure rather than nervous, and this makes it easier to interact with you. If sweaty palms are a regular problem for you, you might try using a special palm antiperspirant designed for golfers and other sports enthusiasts who need a dry grip.

Look, Ma, No Hands

What do you do when the other person doesn't offer a hand? You know you are going to miss out on all the wonderful benefits of the handshake and will have to deal with the awkwardness of establishing rapport without it. If it fits your personality or the situation, you could say as you extend your hand, "I would like to shake your hand." This technique, which I've taught for years, really works. A person who absolutely will not yield to your request is sending you a message. A handshake is a way to share information, establish power, and show respect. Say, for example, you're a sales rep and your prospect does not offer his hand. It may be an indication that he wants to keep the upper hand and dismiss you easily.

Often you can predict the outcome of negotiations, or how difficult they will be, by whether the two parties begin with a handshake. For example, a 1999 *Boston Globe* article reported that, in a reconciliatory talk between Israeli and Palestinian men who had each lost a family member in the Middle Eastern conflict, "the initial greeting was guarded and uneasy. The Israelis took their seats without shaking hands. The Palestinians, seated around a long table, did not stand to greet them. Then both sides started talking."[5] These particular talks ended well, after the participants went beyond their initial signals and offered apologies and forgiveness to one another.

Notice the Handshake Snap You Get and the Snap You Give

1. As you approach someone from a distance to shake hands, notice her eyebrow flash (a quick raising of the eyebrows). The flash signals acknowledgment and precedes the handshake.
2. Observe who puts out the first hand, who lets go first, and how each of these details affects your feelings toward the other person.
3. Pay attention to the kind of handshake you get and the kind you give back.
4. Pay attention to how people respond to your handshake.

(At www.snapfirstimpressions.com, you can participate in a detailed survey on your handshake savvy.)

When Shaking Isn't an Option

Sometimes people avoid shaking hands for religious reasons. Orthodox Jewish men, for example, are not permitted to touch women. Many Muslims have the same intergender prohibition.

I have spoken to physicians, managers, and other health care professionals at a major hospital in Detroit, the city with the highest Muslim population in the country. Hospital staff must deal daily with religious rules forbidding men to touch women. This proscription affects Muslim staff members' interactions with fellow staff, and profoundly affects the ability of male doctors or other male staff to develop a bond of trust with their Muslim and Orthodox Jewish female patients. The no-touch policy originates in profound religious belief, so what do you do?

In this case, because their uncertainty about what to do, as well as their fear of taboo, makes most people freeze, I recommend that staff members be careful of pulling back as they are introduced, or of standing too far away and freezing. They should instead go toward the Muslim or Orthodox Jewish patient and stand no more than two feet away, have extended face-to-face interaction for at least seven seconds, and allow trust to develop. We need to slow down the greeting process to create enough time for each person to feel safe and comfortable in the relationship. If you are in any face-to-face situation where you can't shake hands, follow these recommendations. And if you're a physician or health care professional, or a manager in any setting, know that, by coming into a room and sitting down rather than standing, you appear less threatening, more professional, and more caring, and you are more likely to be heard and understood.

Handshake Alternatives: Cool Greetings and Good-Byes and What They Mean

Is the handshake obsolete? Remember, the handshake means "I come in peace." By refusing to shake hands, whether in the boardroom, in the courtroom, or on the playing field, opponents have no way to establish a relationship outside of the adversarial relationship. Without the handshake at the beginning and end of a meeting or game, situations can become more dangerous. Rapport is not established. Animosities do not get left behind. Greeting rituals allow us to create a positive first impression and connect; if you don't shake hands or perform an alternative ritual, there is a cost.

While the use of the handshake is declining (but hopefully not dying out completely), alternatives to the handshake exist. Not all of these greetings permit the same first-impression rapport building, because they lack the chemical exchange of palm-to-palm contact. However, these alternatives to the traditional handshake can be a significant symbol of friendship and group connection, especially among people who have already developed rapport. Understanding what alternative greeting rituals mean and how to partake in them can give you insight and "club membership" in initial interactions. The following are the most common alternative greeting rituals.

The Dap

The dap — two fists bumped together, knuckle to knuckle — originated in the battlefields of the Vietnam War. However, the dap was not just a way of showing friendship. The fist-to-fist tap symbolized "We are in this fight together." In addition, if the other guy knew the "secret greeting ritual," it helped to distinguish friend from foe.

The fist is a battle symbol — "I have power, and I am willing and able to fight." Two fists moving toward each other symbolize determination and power. As I mentioned earlier, "up" body language, like the winner's upraised arms at the end of a race, symbolizes victory and joy, as when the arm raises up in victory after a mighty battle. When two or more people raise their fists in unison, it is a symbol of unity and creates the feeling that "we will win this together."

During Barack Obama's 2008 presidential campaign, news outlets showed photos of him and Michelle Obama doing the dap. The couple bumped their fists horizontally when they learned he had enough delegates to claim the nomination. As their fists touched, their arms were on an equal level. He was not dapping down to her. They looked at each other eye-to-eye. The horizontal position of their fists, their arms held at an equal level, their eye contact, and their smiles demonstrated the equality of their relationship, as well as joy over the recent victory and a continued commitment to keep fighting.

How to do the dap: Raise your hand as if you're about to shake in the traditional way, but curl your fingers into a fist. Keeping the arm parallel to the floor, little finger down, thumb on top, extend your fist from about chest level and gently tap the other person's fist. For a low, horizontal, fist-meeting, equal-buddy dap, simply rotate your fist ninety degrees, so that the curled fingers are facing the ground, and bump.

(For photos and videos go to "Cool Handshake Alternatives" at www.snapfirstimpressions.com.)

The Thumb-over-Thumb Wrist Wrap

My friend Pat was researching her new novel that takes place in the 1960s, and she talked to me about this handshake variation. She saw it over and over again in newsreels and photos. The thumb-over-thumb wrist wrap, in which you grab the other person's hand above the wrist and end with a thumb lock, was developed by the counterculture of the 1960s when peace activists and youth in general needed a way to differentiate themselves from the dominant culture. These days, you may see it with a complex set of variations and combined with other movements, but the message and ritual meaning are the same: "We are different from the other guys."

One of my clients is an Internet security company. Chris Klaus, a self-proclaimed nerd in his youth, founded the company with fellow nerds when he was a sophomore in college. When I started consulting with the company, I noticed that some of the employees had a thumb-over-thumb wrist wrap variation. The guys told me that when they first got started, they felt like they were "outsider nerds" in a big, corporate suit-and-tie world. The secret ritual they used to greet one another at the beginning of the workday and outside meetings made them feel like they could take on the world. In 2006, the company was sold to IBM for $1.3 billion. I guess the secret handshake worked!

The Chest Bump

The source of this handshake alternative is unknown. Some believe it was first done between African tribesmen as they danced and moved together to gain energy and courage before battle. Most likely you have seen its more modern version in professional sports, especially since the 1990s.

The chest bump symbolizes both vulnerability and elation. Chest bumpers jump up, showing jubilation. They throw their arms out to the side and spread their hands open, revealing that they have no weapons. They push up and out with their chests, exposing and touching hearts, showing that they feel safe being vulnerable and want to join hearts. The powerful smashing movement as the chests meet allows both the joy and the testosterone to surge. It is a cool combination: hearts touching with a smash. For men — and most chest bumpers are male — the move says, "I love you, buddy, but in a manly-man way." Because the ritual is for "bosom buddies," don't try it with someone you've just met!

How to do the chest bump: Approach your chest-bumping partner, pull your shoulders back and extend your arms, palms open, to the side. Jump forward and bump your partner's chest.

The High Five

The high five developed in the 1970s as an extension of the handshake. While the handshake can be sterile and perfunctory, the high five symbolizes joy, elation, and power. It is very different from the dap. Since in the high five the palm is open and the fingers are spread out, it conveys an open, unadulterated win — in other words, "We have got it made." You can see it as a simple victory gesture when you watch any basketball game. The players often glance at the hands and then look away immediately, indicating it is merely a victory move, not a greeting-bonding ritual. You may have noticed that men give toddler boys high fives. The high five initiates the small boys into the joy of play that is part of being a guy. The handshake, in contrast, symbolizes for some men their entry into the adult world, especially the corporate world.

How to do the high five: Raise your hand above your head and, showing your open palm, slap the hand of your partner. The louder the slap, the better.

The Peace Sign, or Victory V

My friend Carl is a biker. He is smart and cool, and he greets fellow bikers on the road with a peace sign. Who knew that the hippie greeting would still be cool today? The V is important not just because it is a universally recognized hand gesture that identifies someone who comes in peace; for some it is also a show of forceful victory over others and signifies brotherhood — in Carl's case, the brotherhood of bikers.

Remember, we like people who are like us. The various versions of the peace symbol given by bikers show other bikers that they have something in common. Bikers will slightly raise their fingers off the handlebars in the peace sign to greet fellow riders, especially those riding the same bike brand or using the same type of helmet.[6] A stronger greeting signifying full brotherhood occurs when the full hand and arm come off the handles and the rider gives the peace sign with the V tilted sideways. What we consider to be the peace sign is not recognized everywhere.

If your palm is facing inward as you make the V sign to someone in the United Kingdom, Ireland, New Zealand, or Australia, you may be met with a nasty look. That gesture is considered an insult in those countries. Some cultures view an upraised V sign as an obscene gesture along the lines of flipping someone the bird in this country. It may have its origins in sexual symbolism, or it may communicate a desire to fight. In the 1300s, the V sign symbolized the drawing of a bow about to shoot an arrow.

War and Peace

During World War II, Victor de Laveleye, a Belgian refugee, suggested while doing a shortwave broadcast that his countrymen use the letter *V* as a rallying sign. *V* is the first letter of *victoire* (victory) in French and *vrijheid* (freedom) in Dutch. Soon you could see the *V* in graffiti painted all over Belgium, and then all over Nazi-occupied Europe. Then it was also given as a hand sign. It was a message that let the occupier know that he was "surrounded, encircled by an immense crowd of citizens eagerly awaiting his first moment of weakness."[7]

Also during World War II, British prime minister Winston Churchill popularized the V symbol throughout the world as a symbol of victory. You can find iconic photos of him holding his fingers in a V with his palm facing out. Like the Belgian symbol, it was a greeting ritual to help people in wartime feel victorious.

In 1958, the British artist Gerald Holtom began using a graphic representation of the V as a symbol of peace rather than victory through battle.[8] Eventually, the anti–nuclear war and anti–Vietnam War movements adopted the V as a sign for peace and love. More recently, it generated controversy in the Middle East when Palestinians raised the V sign and Israelis and others debated whether it symbolized victory or peace. Some argued that it symbolized *hudna*, an Arabic term meaning "a temporary truce." Others argued that it meant Palestinians wanted time to pause instead of attacking, or that they desired lasting peace. Yes, a simple greeting ritual can mean so much.

Carol and Jeff are friends of mine who broke up under less-than-amicable circumstances. Battle lines were formed and the ownership of everything from flat-screen televisions to friendships was argued. A year later, both were invited to a backyard barbecue. As he came through the door, Jeff first popped his smiling face toward Carol and then raised a peace sign. Her returning smile and hearty laugh let him know he was safe.

Flashing the peace sign in North America today can send a first impression that is sometimes hip, sometimes humorous or nostalgic, and sometimes a request for openness. It is a greeting that shows others your own beliefs and desires and asks in return, "Are you part of my tribe? Will you interact with me in harmony?"

How to do the V peace sign: Hold your hand up, palm facing forward. Curl the thumb, ring, and little finger inward, leaving the index and middle finger extended to form a V.

Man Hugs

In the 1980s, twenty years after the feminist movement encouraged women to embrace their stronger, traditionally male side, men began their own revolution. Men began to embrace one another to show their softer side. Before this, the only time you typically saw men in North America hugging was when they played sports, attended a funeral, or got married.

I have seen an increase in male hugging ever since two HBO TV series, *The Sopranos* and *Entourage*, showed that real men could hug as long as they gave the "man hug." I first noticed the man hug being exchanged by the male athletes in my communication classes at Auburn University. The young men would see a fellow athlete in the hallway or on the campus green and want to give a hug of warmth and friendship, but they were out in public view. People were watching. So they would give a combination handshake-hug. In the handshake-hug, the men first stick out one hand for a handshake and then, with their right hands locked in the handshake (to keep the two participants from getting too close), wrap the left arm around the other's shoulder and hug. The two men hug with only their upper bodies touching and their lower torsos held out and away. Finally, to ensure that no one can misconstrue this partial hug as a sissy move, each takes the hand that he briefly held against the other's back and pounds the back hard three or four times.

In fact, you could tell if the men were close buddies. They would strike each other *harder*, just to show how much they cared! Men showing affection through hitting says, "I love you, guy, but not that way." Unlike the traditional hug, which symbolically and effectively brings people into the intimate zone of space, removes barriers, and unites the two persons embracing, this pounding hug brings only the upper torso into intimate proximity. The aggressive act of striking the back ensures that each man knows the other is still a testosterone-rich, card-carrying member of the "man club."

The man hug, or pound hug, is exclusively performed between two males. It also goes by other names, including *pound shake*, *dude hug*, *shug*, or *bro hug*. It's a greeting or parting ritual that demonstrates a certain level of intimacy typically reserved for close friends and family.

While the different names for the man hug have entered the lexicon, the meaning of the hug has expanded to cover other things as well. Men can now "hug it out" in other circumstances. First heard by the masses decades ago in an episode of *Friends* on TV, the phrase *hug it out* means that one person, typically a male, gives another person, typically another male, a pound hug to help the man get through a difficult or sad situation. Instead of being a spontaneous show of affection, this hug is preceded by a request for permission before it is given. So the exchange sounds something like this:

Guy 1: "Man, my girlfriend just dumped me."

Guy 2: "Do you wanna hug it out?"

In an episode of *Entourage*, two of the guys are in a screaming argument on an elevator. Once the doors open and they are in public view, one guy turns to the other and says, "Wanna hug it out?" In this use, the pound hug, preceded by the phrase "Wanna hug it out," means "Hey, we were arguing, but now that we are in public, let's show we are friends for now. Then we can continue this later in private." The phrase "Let's hug it out" means "Let's be friends again" after an argument, or when one man feels he has insulted another.

The Plain Old Hug

While I was teaching body language and nonverbal communication at Florida State University, students coming up to me before and after class, or running into me on campus, would inevitably open their arms to receive a hug. Perhaps they were motivated by my quoting research on the benefits of touch. In addition, the professional people who attended my speeches and training sessions would recognize me in a restaurant or the grocery store checkout line and typically meet me with a warm and friendly hug.

A hug fully crosses the intimate-zone boundaries of the body, while other greetings, from the handshake to the bow to the upheld palms in a high five, are designed to keep people apart and outside the intimate zero-to-eighteen-inch zone. A hug is a greeting of friend to friend.

You may think of the hug as only a touchy-feely greeting. It may surprise you to learn that the hug actually originated in Egypt as a way for men meeting strangers to check for swords hidden under their long robes. It continued as a "Let me pat you down" weapons check in Arab greetings (and on TV cop shows and at airport security). Only in the past century has the full frontal hug morphed into the embrace showing warmth and affection. This full face-to-face hug shows others that we trust them and are willing to give them ready and full access to our vulnerable hearts.

While people are avoiding handshakes, hugging seems to be increasing in popularity. Some say the increase came after the tragedy of 9/11 as the need for comfort and bonding increased. Others say the switch to casual dress in corporate America in the first decade of the twenty-first century brought a desire for a more casual greeting ritual. I feel it is a response in some parts of the country to the positive influence of Latin cultures that hug, and a response to the negative influence of a high-tech culture, in which we have so little touch and few physical connections with others.

Do Queens Hug?

At the end of 2009, Michelle Obama gave Queen Elizabeth a hug at Buckingham Palace. This lack of formality broke royal protocol. The British newspaper the *Guardian*, reporting on the incident, noted, however, that Ms. Obama was not the "first person to have initiated physical contact with Elizabeth without ending up in the Tower. At least four people are known to have broken this rule."[9] Queen Elizabeth was surprised at Ms. Obama's gesture, and it was a bit awkward. She showed delayed acceptance of this exchange, however, by also breaking protocol and reaching her arm around Ms. Obama's back to return the favor.

My high school and college audiences share with me that hugging makes them feel accepted and loved by their friends in a way they don't feel with their parents. My principal audiences and schoolteacher audiences say that, with two-parent working families, kids hugging each other helps them get the healthy touch they are missing out on at home. I remember fondly the warm, full, heart-to-heart hugs shared with my fellow church group members that we had when I was in high school.

The Hug Dodge

So, you're not a hugger, and this whole hugging thing makes you a little uneasy. There are many motivations for dodging a hug, and more than one method to do it. It was front-page news in the Irish press when Bono, of the rock group U2, admitted that he had dodged a hug from then president George W. Bush by jumping behind a podium as the affectionate Bush came near him. Bono said he didn't feel like being the recipient of a hug from someone he disagreed with on so many things.

I'm a hugger, so I don't worry about people hugging me. But I know there have been times when someone didn't want to hug me. Not everyone is a hugger. When you hug, you expose the front of your body, opening all your body windows. It can make some people feel vulnerable. Others feel that hugs are too personal and intimate and even too sexual for everyday interactions in business and with acquaintances. Thankfully, their body language cues will let you know very quickly whether they are huggers.

Carol, a sales rep in my sales presentation skills class, asked, "What if I don't want a hug? Some of the clients I call on immediately give me a hug, and I am just not into that." This is a question that women in business frequently ask. The good news, for Carol and all the "I am not a hugger" people, is that there is a systematic technique for avoiding the hug. See the sidebar "Hug Dodge Instructions."

Macey, a drop-dead gorgeous client of mine, came in for a coaching session after receiving the hug dodge training in our previous session. She said, "I feel so empowered. Yesterday I was at a meeting. My boss's boss, who goes in for the really uncomfortable, feel-you-up kind of hug, approached me with his arms out at the meeting. I was able to use the hug dodge to change it to a much more comfortable handshake. I realized at once how powerless and uncomfortable I typically feel when I have to interact with him after one of his inappropriately sexual hugs."

Hug Dodge Instructions

If you see the potential hugger with both hands and arms raised and chest thrust out in the "hug" position, do the following:

1. Break eye contact.
2. Step forward on your right foot (this is your "handshaking foot," the foot that normally moves first when you go in for a handshake).
3. Present only the right side of your body, which effectively closes off your body windows
4. Extend your right hand for a handshake. (You can choose to make eye contact again at this point.)
5. After touching, step back outside the intimate zone of space to signal you are done, and that you don't want to follow the handshake with a hug. This step also sends the signal that, not only is the hug unwanted now, but it is also unwanted in the future.

If extending your arm and presenting your right side doesn't stop the hugger, wrap your left arm around the person's shoulder. This way it becomes a side-to-side hug rather than a frontal hug. You can also pat his back or shoulder to ensure that you indicate you don't want a sexual interaction.

The hug dodge does two things: It signals in those important first milliseconds that you are initiating a handshake interaction. And it closes and protects the windows of your body.

Know Your Hug-ee

Whether a hug is appropriate often depends on a person's perception of what's good and bad. As people have become more aware, and phobic about even politically correct and gender-appropriate touch, some people often find a hug or kiss uncomfortable because they perceive or fear some sexual intent. Women have shared with me that a guy may press his chest against a woman's breasts too closely (on purpose or not), or put his pelvis against a woman's body, or that he might linger too long in a hug.

Men have seldom told me that hugging a woman was uncomfortable. Those who have, said it was because they didn't know the woman that well.

Female salespeople tend to have the biggest problem with inappropriate hugs — from clients. In sales, people sometimes like to hug and kiss to show that the relationship goes beyond business. It's a way of saying, "Hey, I am not just here to sell to you. We have a real friendship."

Awkward kisses given with a hug can be avoided using the hug dodge moves. Of course, a kiss can be more difficult to combat than a hug if the kiss is an accepted cultural greeting ritual. Avoiding this tradition could cost the salesperson or businessperson some very important business. For instance, the French like to do a triple kiss. They kiss you on one cheek, then the other, and then the first cheek again. In Latin American countries they might kiss twice, then hug. You have to know where you are and with whom you are interacting, and weigh the benefits and the costs.

If you're a hugger, please realize that the moves people make to avoid hugs are the same ones you should keep an eye out for so you don't force someone into an unwanted embrace. Watch for the eyes dropping down and closed body windows.

EXERCISE

Test Your Handshakes

Notice how people in your life who come from different cultures, religions, ages, backgrounds, and interests, as well as people in the media, greet each other. Try a few of the cool handshake alternatives described in this chapter, and note the result. Ask people if they have noticed changes in the way we greet each other.

—ⅉ—

When we meet and approach others, a wealth of nonverbal behaviors affects our snap impressions. We turn to some of those in the next chapter.

4. THE FACE OF FIRST IMPRESSIONS

Reading and Improving Aspects of Facial Expressions beyond Just Making Eye Contact and Smiling

It was Valentine's Day, and I was stuck in a snowstorm in a very crowded Chicago airport. Standing in the long security line, and scanning the crowd around me, I noticed that a man behind me was glancing at me and then glancing away. The glances were a beat longer than normal glances. The repetition of the glances told me the man was interested in me. He sent the message in a way that wasn't pushy or forward. I thought, "How nice." It was an invitation, but I didn't glance back.

Remembering that I had a bottle of water in my carry-on, I pulled it out and opened it. The water was carbonated and sprayed all over me, leaving me soaking wet and laughing. I glanced at the guy behind me thinking, "Now he will look away because I look like a dork!" Instead, he looked right at me and locked into my gaze. He smiled and laughed with me. We talked our way through the security line, matching glances and smiles. It was "in like" at first sight, and on that February 14 we became Valentines.

In this chapter you'll discover how eye contact, smiles, and over-all facial expressions affect the first impressions we make on others. You'll also learn steps for improving those first impressions and reading others' expressions.

Eye Contact

Eye contact greatly affects the first impressions you make on strangers and the impressions you make at the beginnings of interactions with people you know. Your "eye impressions" determine how people see you. An eye impression is a small behavior with a big impact on your snap. For example, a new manager complained to me that his employees didn't seem to take his assignments seriously. "Either they hand them in late or they don't hand them in at all and I end up doing all their work!" While coaching this new manager on employee interactions, I noticed that his body was turned toward me. But as I played an employee, he talked to me without connecting to my eyes. Instead, he looked at the document in his hands, pointing out tasks to me. As he talked about details and deadlines, he looked at everything but my eyes — his shoes, my shoes, the wall behind me.

Working together, we discovered this was not just because he was nervous at the beginning of coaching. It was his habitual way of interacting with his employees. The employees weren't following through because he was not connecting with them. His eye contact — or lack of contact — was actually submissive. No one felt the need to take his directives seriously.

The impressions you make with your eyes can determine other people's response to you. In this case, the manager's gaze indicated a lack of power and confidence. Your gaze gives you control of the conversation, whether you are the speaker or the listener. To build rapport, you need to gaze at that person

60 to 70 percent of the time while listening, and 40 percent of the time while talking, intermittently looking away.[1] Making eye contact sends the message that you are serious and confident in yourself, and that you believe in what you're saying.

If you saw a house with windows boarded up, you typically wouldn't go in; you have read too many scary Stephen King novels to do that! When you don't make eye contact, you are like the house with the boarded windows. "The eyes are the windows to the soul" is an often-quoted metaphor for a reason. Just as a window opens your house to the outside, your eye contact opens you to people. Eye impressions affect our credibility, arouse our emotions, and signal our intent. While different cultures interpret eye contact differently, it's always a significant part of each person's snap.

Eye Tests

Imagine you are a supervisor. Your department has grown and you need to select an employee to take on more responsibility. You know the person you choose will need leadership abilities. You have narrowed your search to four equally talented employees. In talking with them, you find they are saying the right things, but you notice their eye contact varies significantly.

Employee A has an unblinking stare with contracted (small) pupils.

Employee B is looking at you approximately half the time when he is speaking and about 75 percent of the time when you are speaking. He tends to focus on your eyes and the bridge of your nose.

Employee C looks at you normally (60 to 70 percent of the time). Her gaze tends to hover at your mouth and nose. When you talk about working longer hours and supervising others, her blinking rate increases.

Employee D looks at you about half the time with her gaze

focusing on your eyes and nose. Occasionally her eyelids flatten out slightly when you're talking.

Which one would you choose? Let's unpack the secrets of these eye contact factors, cues that we subconsciously respond to all the time. Remember, your eyes "speak" as loudly as your voice. We subconsciously watch other people's eye behavior to predict what they will do next.[2] During a high-stakes poker game on television, for example, a game featuring professional players, one of the players is wearing sunglasses. Is it a showy prop? Or do the glasses give him an advantage? Research shows professional poker players win fewer games when their opponents wear dark glasses. The reason? They can't observe their opponent's eyes, which clue them in on his next move. I am surprised these glasses are even allowed in professional games, because they give the wearer a proven advantage over other players! To me, it's like using steroids in an athletic contest.

Studies on eye contact and its effect on communication and credibility find that maintaining a steady gaze while communicating promotes credibility.[3] Conversely, averting eye contact is detrimental to credibility. Eye-contact studies have produced information about the effect of eye contact on the three components of credibility we've discussed: dynamism, competence, and trustworthiness. In tests where these three components were isolated, eye behavior did little to produce the effect of dynamism. The appearance of competence and trustworthiness, however, was significantly linked to eye behavior.

When volunteers were asked to rate the competence of communicators with low eye contact and with high eye contact, the competence ratings were significantly higher for the subjects who exhibited high eye contact with the audience. The same test produced the same results in measuring trustworthiness.

The six muscles that work together to move each eyeball are common to all vertebrate animals. The muscles' nerves link to the unconscious as well as to the thinking parts of our brains. We consciously control where our own eyes hover and land, but our eyes have some primal hard wiring, as well, that makes them look at things that are interesting, especially faces. We tend to look away from ugly or distasteful things. And we look down or away from people at times, as part of our primal wiring, because an intense gaze could signal a desire to attack. Numerous studies have shown that an unwavering gaze in primates evolved as a sign of dominance and threat, while gaze avoidance evolved as a submissive cue.

How to Be Charismatic

The one consistent nonverbal behavior I find in highly charismatic people is laser-focused eye contact. Years ago, I made an appearance on the *Live with Regis and Kelly* show to talk about how couples' sleep positions can show what is going on in their relationships. While I was, so to speak, in bed with Regis (I love saying that!) on the studio set, I discovered that he is incredibly charismatic. His focused eye contact is amazing. The eye contact started before the show as he asked me questions and listened attentively amid the audience and backstage noise. During commercial breaks, he kept this laser-focused gaze directly on my eyes, as if I were the only person on the planet, the center of the universe. I was, I admit, mesmerized. This kind of focus makes its recipient feel seen, heard, and understood. I have found in my work that this is the most common description of nonverbal behavior that people give when they describe someone they have met who is charismatic.

Making eye contact is the most powerful way of establishing contact with another person. Think of eye-to-eye contact as a battery charger; unless you plug into the other person, there is no charge between you. Your mouth is moving, but he can't and

won't hear you. Whenever you meet someone, it's your responsibility to plug in.

Eye contact has an effect on everyone you interact with.
Research shows that a listener's good eye contact makes the
speaker more animated in her delivery. Even research on eye contact in video conference calls shows that people in group discussions will speak up more often if they receive a greater amount
of eye contact from other group members, whether the eye contact is made while the subject is speaking or made randomly.[4]

In addition, making eye contact with someone can make it
easier for her to understand what you are feeling. Eye contact
seems to act as an invitation for mimicry, triggering mecha-
nisms in the frontal region of
the brain that control imitation.[5]
Think about the last meeting you
attended and which individuals
made eye contact. How did this
affect how the meeting went?

In another example, Jane had
a positive interview with Claire,
the human resources director at
a firm that was hiring. Jane had
been nervous — who isn't before
an interview? — but Claire gave
her a welcoming smile and good
eye contact. Because Claire's eyes
lit up as Jane relayed her work
experience, and even seemed to
smile when Jane showed she'd thoroughly researched the job
and the company, Jane was able to be her best, most natural self.

When Jane was called back in to interview with three of
the managers she'd be working with on the job, the managers
greeted her but then looked down at notes and their copies

**What Does That
Lingering Glance Mean?**

Increasing your eye contact with
someone can

- make conversation more lively
  by increasing animation;
- help people in one-on-one and
  group settings to open up and
  share;
- help others understand your
  feelings;
- show that you are listening
  and empathetic; and
- allow you to connect more
  quickly and deeply with
  others.

of her résumé. When they asked questions, they continued to read and look down or at each other. Luckily, Claire was in the room. As Jane floundered a bit, she looked at Claire, saw interest and encouragement in her eyes, and was able to shift back into the self she'd been in their earlier interview. (See chapter 8 for much more on job interviews.) The takeaway: Look for what I call the "goodie" person. The goodie person makes eye contact with you, which translates as acceptance.

EXERCISE

Charismatic Eye Contact

Notice how others make eye contact with you this week.

- Who makes you feel seen, heard, and understood?
- What do these people do to create this effect, and can you model it?
- Is there someone you feel is charismatic? Watch his eye contact. Study the length of his gaze when he is speaking and listening.
- Watch a few talk shows or one-on-one news interviews. Look for interviews in which you can see the interviewer and the guest in one shot, and study how the best interviewers look at their guests.

It's Not Polite to Stare

There is distinct difference between charismatic eye contact that shows someone is focused on you as you interact and someone who is glaring at you as if she is starving and you're a juicy burger.

If people find you overbearing, I'll bet your eye contact is part of the problem. If you look too long and don't break away enough, it's intimidating. As the speaker, you want to gaze, not stare. If you gaze more than the recognized standard of 70 percent of the time, people are going to think you're a bully or weird — or that they have spinach between their teeth. A participant in my first-impressions workshop came up to me after the program and said, "I don't understand. Women don't seem to like me. I don't have trouble going up to women and starting a conversation, but they seem really uncomfortable. Some even make a face or walk away. I have read all the stuff online about flirting, but I can't figure out what I am doing wrong."

Interestingly, I had noticed his snap issue moments after he entered the classroom. He held eye contact with attractive women far too long. He was not glancing; he was staring. It felt like an assault rather than an "invitation to dance." Until we spoke, he had no idea that his eye contact was aggressive.

This is actually an issue I have encountered with several male coaching clients. If you have eye-contact issues, go deep and explore what emotions you are feeling. You may be blaming other people for the reaction they are giving you for a behavior you're not aware of. So dig a little. I have worked with coaching clients who came to realize they glared at coworkers because deep down, they were angry about their workload, or perhaps even about past issues unrelated to their current workplace.

We Teach Our Children Well

When my nephew Craig was born, our family would gather in any room he was in and look at him, play peekaboo with him, and generally gaze into his baby blues with what our family now fondly calls "baby worship." Craig is grown now, with a baby of his own named Simon. We repeat what we did when Craig was born: we all gladly sit on the floor, bow down, and coo to Simon's big blue eyes.

Baby Simon loves this. He lights up, his mouth drops open, and he laughs. It's great. Everywhere we go, whether a restaurant, the drugstore, or a shop, or while simply walking down the street, people stop to give baby worship to little Simon. Recently, Craig and his wife and six-month-old Simon went to California, which required two long plane trips. Craig told me, "Patti, it was the funniest thing. We would get on the plane, and Simon would be smiling. He would try to make eye contact with the people around us. They wouldn't look at him. He would try and try, but no matter where he looked, people would look down and away. They were probably thinking, 'Oh God. I am sitting near a baby who is going to be crying for the next four hours!'"

Simon became frustrated because he was used to making the snap connection. He was smart enough to know that eye contact worked, and now nobody would give him his well-deserved baby worship! Little Simon had an infant eye-contact advantage, though. Infants blink less — as little as once or twice a minute — so their eye contact is more intense. That's okay because babies are not threatening.

The Wisdom of Babes

From birth, infants prefer to look at faces that are looking at them. Two-to-five-day-old babies can discriminate between direct and averted gaze. We begin to love mutual gazes early in life. Healthy babies show more activity in the brain in response to a direct gaze than to a glance. Some researchers theorize that if you play with your baby in games involving a mutual

The Baby Brain

In her controversial book *The Female Brain*, neuropsychiatrist Louann Brizendine emphasizes that, before birth, baby girls' brains are wired differently than those of boys. She describes how girl infants "come out wired for mutual gazing," and says, "over the first three months of life, a baby girl's skills in eye contact and mutual face gazing will increase by over 400 percent, whereas facial gazing skills in boys during this time will not increase at all. Baby girls are born interested in emotional expression."[6]

gaze, you help grow the baby's brain. Mutual gazing — literally and figuratively being "seen" — actually facilitates the brain's development.[7]

Pediatricians say that, to increase a baby's ability to make eye contact, you can wave your hands in front of your eyes, or wear funny eye makeup, big, clown-like false eyelashes, or funny glasses, to direct the child to look you in the eyes. You can give an extrabig smile when the child makes direct eye contact, or you can give her a toy or small bit of soft candy if she is old enough to chew. Most important, make an eye connection with your baby.

What Different Eye Behavior Means

There are so many meanings gleaned from different eye behaviors, and many things to pay attention to. Let's look at some variations in how we gaze at others, and talk about when to use these variations and how they affect the way others see you; see if you should add or subtract them from your repertoire.

Triangle Gazes

Eye contact arouses our emotions. Our breathing rate and heart rate go up, and if eye contact is maintained for too long, our palms sweat. Mutual gazes, with both parties looking at exactly the same part of the eyes, rarely last longer than three seconds before one or both people have the urge to break the contact by glancing down or away. That's why we use a triangle gaze: breaking eye contact lowers our stress levels.

To give you an example of the degree to which eye contact can vary from culture to culture, in Japan listeners are taught to focus on a speaker's neck in order to avoid eye contact, as direct eye contact is considered rude.

(For videos of the different types of gazes, go to www.snap firstimpressions.com.)

Upper-Triangle Gaze

In business conversations, you should focus mainly on the other person's eyes whether you are speaking or listening. A trick to looking powerful or to maintaining control is to keep your eyes in the triangle formed by the other's eyes and the area just above the bridge of her nose.

Middle-Triangle Gaze

In everyday interpersonal conversation, you should look at the mouth at its base and the nose at its peak. However, if you typically use that as your only focus triangle, and don't ever look at the upper triangle, you'll look submissive.

Bottom-Triangle Gaze

This is a large triangle going from the eyes all the way down to the center of the chest. Let's say you're negotiating with someone and your eyes drop from the upper triangle and stay on the chest of your fellow negotiator as he makes a certain point. You may be sending a signal that you're willing to give in on that point. The bottom-triangle gaze looks like a sign of submission.

Blinking

Our normal blinking rate is twenty closures per minute. If someone blinks even slightly more often than that, it can be a sign he or she is excited or nervous. Even if you are blinking because your eyes are dry or the lights are bright, the interpretation of your blinking may be "I bet she is blinking because she is nervous." By blinking more often, we are symbolically protecting ourselves from the stressful situation. Blinking is like a polygraph test of our arousal. Excitement causes the brain to release dopamine, and that makes us blink faster. Our blinks naturally rise in rate of frequency with anxious or tense topics.

When you're relaxed, the blink rate is ten to twenty-five

blinks per minute. When you're talking, it increases to about twenty to twenty-five blinks per minute. As a blink rate climbs above fifty, and especially when it goes above seventy, it indicates an increased level of stress. Increased blinking is a common occurrence. When someone appears in front of a television camera, blink frequency increases to thirty to fifty times a minute because of "audience stress."

Blinking slowly, so the eyes are closed for up to a second, signals everything from disinterest to superior attitude to boredom. Rapid blinking signals disbelief, lack of acceptance, and occasionally attraction or nervousness.

Eyelash Flutter

When former president Richard M. Nixon gave his 1974 resignation speech on television, he appeared calm, cool, and collected. But he showed episodic bursts of blinking above the fifty-blinks-per-minute cutoff point for normal blinking. This rapid blinking during stress is now called the "Nixon effect," or eyelash flutter, and can increase to more than eighty blinks per minute.

In an eyelash flutter, the eye doesn't close completely and the flutter is incredibly fast. The timing of the flutter is important. A stressful sales call, job interview, or TV interview can cause rapid blinking. If someone blinks rapidly during an entire interview, she may merely be stressed about the interview. But if she doesn't do any rapid blinking at all and, when asked a specific question, doesn't flutter, pay close attention to the answer. When I analyze video of TV interviews and police interrogations, I look for the baseline of someone's normal blink rate, ideally when he is not under stress. If he flutters in response to a particular question, it's an indication that he is uncomfortable with the question and that the next statement he makes might be a lie. In training trial lawyers and mediators,

I suggest they give witnesses or clients several choices. When they see the person's eyes flutter, they've hit the stress spot and have the true answer.

You can use the same technique I use when I train salespeople, managers, and team leaders to find out the true problem or conflict when someone is reticent to share. To get to the truth when speaking to someone, state several possibilities and note when his eyes flutter in response.

How does your blink rate affect first impressions? If you are giving a speech, asking for a phone number, or introducing yourself at a meeting, your blink rate can make you a winner or loser.

When people like what they see, their pupil size increases, and their blink rate may too. When you want someone to know you like her, and you want her to feel more excited around you, try increasing her blink rate as you talk to her. Blink more yourself If the person likes you, she'll unconsciously try to match your blink rate to keep in sync with you, which in turn makes you both feel more attracted to each other. In fact, by mimicking the faster blink rate, your companion will also likely become more excited.

Winners Don't Blink

Since the Nixon effect was first noted, researchers have been using blink rate to analyze speakers. Researcher J. J. Tecce of Boston College found that, "of the seven [U.S.] presidential elections for which televised debates are available, in six elections, the candidate who blinked the most frequently during debates eventually lost the election."[8]

(Check www.snapfirst impressions.com for more ways to read candidates and everyday people, and for videos that show differences in blink rate.)

Sideways Glance

Sideways glances must be examined along with other cues. If someone gives you a sideways glance, looks up, and smiles, he may be saying, "I am interested in you or what you're saying," or simply showing that he is happy. This is different from the involuntary eye movements to the right or left that we make while processing information.

Eye Rub

When people rub their eyes, it can mean that their eyes itch. But it can also indicate that a person is trying to deceive you. Remember from the section on blink rate that the timing is the tell. If someone rubs his eyes and then looks down and away, it's a strong sign that he is lying. If he does it when you are talking, he may not believe you. It also can show a lack of comfort with the topic, as in, "I wish to 'see no evil' so I will rub my eyes."

Eye Roll

Tina was sent to my three-day interpersonal skills class with the message that new clients said she was rude and disrespectful in her snap impression. Her coaching partner in the first workshop team exercise nailed one eye behavior that contributed to the bad impression she made: Tina rolled her eyes whenever she was listening to anyone making a factual statement. Her partner counted five eye rolls in three minutes. When coached, Tina exclaimed, "Oh my God. I can't stand it when anyone sounds pompous. But I had no idea I rolled my eyes when anyone just sounds smart!"

We've all been in situations in which we're explaining something to somebody and he rolls his eyes. If watching him do so makes you feel inferior, your feeling is on target: that's what he believes in that moment. An eye roll is a dismissive gesture that indicates superiority. It's a particularly common behavior in teenagers.

Breaking Eye Contact

Neurolinguistic programming techniques say that people indicate what they're thinking by where they look — up or down and to the right or the left. What you might not know is that the least intimidating way to break eye contact in a good conversation is to look down. Notice how you tend to break eye contact when you make a snap impression. Breaking by looking down shows submission. It's not going to make you look powerful, but it will make people feel more comfortable around you and increase their self-disclosure.

Staring

Being stared at arouses the sympathetic nervous system and can make the freeze-flight-fight-or-faint response kick in. When a person stares with large pupils, it can mean the person wants to attract you — or just plain wants you. We usually think of eye contact as showing interest, but that's not always the case. An unblinking stare, with contracted (small) pupils, means the person is actually not interested in what you are saying or doesn't agree with your views.

**Twelve Eye-Contact Tips to Improve
the First Impressions You Make**

1. Think of staring eyes as being similar to upraised hands. A look that lasts too long is like upraised hands forming into fists begging for a fight.

2. You're a woman and you are talking to a man you know. Perhaps he is a client or coworker, a friend or a sweetie. As you talk, he is conversing but not looking at you. Instead, he looks forward toward your project on the desk or table, or forward toward the TV screen. You think, "He is not looking at me while we talk." But men, as a gender, can focus on the conversation without making eye contact. Actually, they may prefer it. It can signal camaraderie and cooperation, whereas eye-to-eye contact can engage the freeze-flight-fight-or-faint response.

3. While making eye contact is typically the best behavior for listening, looking away or closing your eyes while listening is a natural process that can occasionally be helpful, as it can keep you from being distracted by visual stimulation. Just as I have noticed that adults with ADD will cross their arms to focus — to close down distractions while listening — I have also noticed that people over the age of sixty-five, and people who have slight hearing problems, will look away to listen. It may seem counterintuitive, but the lack of eye contact helps you focus on the words and the paralanguage.

4. When someone is lying, her eyes will meet yours less than 30 percent of the time, but as we've discussed, a lack of eye contact does not necessarily indicate lying. Moreover, a liar can look you straight in the eye. In fact, pathological liars are great at making eye contact.

5. Whether you're a man or a woman, to make a woman more comfortable in initial interactions, try to keep your eye contact sightline slightly below hers. This means you should adopt the middle-triangle gaze. This is critically important if you're a man trying to make a woman with less power feel important or more at ease. Straight eye-to-eye contact can seem too aggressive.

6. When speaking one-on-one, vary your eye contact. You may want to maintain eye contact with your partner by looking from one eye to the other, not with the swinging regularity of a metronome, but as though you were planting a message in each eye. This is actually an eye-contact behavior we do subconsciously when we are listening intensely; it conveys sincerity.

7. When we type an email to a friend, we may add boldface to a word to show we really mean it, or that the word

is really important. We use our voices and gestures to emphasize words as well, but a more subtle cue to look for is the widening of the eyes when a particular word is spoken. The brow and/or the eyelid raises, and the lower part of the eyelid lowers. This cue acts as nonverbal italics or boldface. Blinking can be a similar indicator. If you watch someone carefully, you'll see him blink at the start or end of an important word. This gives the word a special emphasis.

8. There are times you may want to maintain a good impression but shorten a particular interaction. The next time you're at a meeting or party, notice how people verbally greet, shake hands, or embrace and then step back and look away. Anthropologist Adam Kendon calls this "the cutoff."[9] He believes we use this as a way of maintaining equilibrium when neither person involved has power over the other. If you think about it, there is a certain acceptable level of touch and length of hug time and gaze time when you greet your friends and acquaintances, based on the level of intimacy you have with each other. If you don't follow this little ritual, and look at each other too long, it feels uncomfortable. Some kind of cutoff is needed after a greeting so that everything can quickly get back to normal.

9. When you're listening to coaching and feedback, as well as to criticism, it is normal to want to break eye contact and listen while looking down. But looking down might make the speaker think you are not listening. Instead, as you listen, maintain normal look/ look-away eye contact. Looking down less often makes you look confident and professional and, according to research, is likely to shorten the length of the criticism

because the speaker knows you are listening to and accepting the information.

10. Gazing down can mean defeat or reflect guilt, shame, or submissiveness. When we are startled, gazing down quickly is a reflexive response. In interrogation or when listening to answers on the witness stand, police officers and lawyers look for where the suspect's gaze goes as he professes to be innocent. If he says, "I am innocent" and immediately glances down and away, the suspect is not confident of his own innocence. When telling the truth, we tend to gaze at normal face-to-face level and hold the gaze for three seconds or longer.

11. Suddenly narrowed, or slitted, eyes may reveal disagreement or uncertainty. Our brains are actually protecting us from the discomfort of hearing a disagreeable message by a quick tightening of the eye that hides the eye under lowered hoods.

    In research on eye contact in job interviews, researchers found that candidates with nonassertive eyes (defined as averted, downcast, teary, or pleading) or aggressive eyes (identified as narrowed, cold, or staring) were rated significantly lower than candidates with assertive eyes (open, frank, and direct).[10]

12. When we first see someone we're attracted to, our eyebrows rise and fall. If she is similarly attracted, she raises her eyebrows in return. Never noticed? It's not surprising, since the onset of the eyebrow flash typically follows a pause in all other facial movements but takes only about one hundred milliseconds to have any impact. The eyebrow flash is consistent across cultures in muscle action and timing, in concert with other

facial movements, including the raising of the lips in a smile and the lifting of the upper lid.[11]

What if you struggle to maintain eye contact? Many people do, and there are many reasons why this happens. It can be a result of your personality type, past experiences, or even your genetic makeup.[12] Here are some thoughts on what you can do. First, ask yourself why you feel you're struggling. Do you feel scared, overpowered, stressed, or shy when you make eye contact? Breaking eye contact or resisting making eye contact temporarily reduces the information coming into the brain and therefore stops emotions from escalating. It's like turning down the lights when they're too bright. You may be breaking eye contact to regain control of your emotional state. So before stressful interactions, ask yourself, "What is the worst thing that can happen? Will they walk away? Notice I am shy? Boil me in oil?"

Then, if you're still struggling with eye contact, split your attention and look in turn at the person's mouth, eyes, and cheeks. In our everyday interactions, we normally split our gaze like that, though we spend the most time looking at others' eyes. Splitting your gaze is more natural and makes the lack of eye contact less obvious.

EXERCISE

Check Your Choice

Go back to the four employees — A, B, C, and D — that I mentioned earlier in the chapter (pages 95-96) as candidates for a job promotion. Reassess your choice and see if the information we've covered in the chapter has changed your mind. You'll soon discover the employee who deserves the promotion.

Smiles

While the eyes "have it," there's more than just eye contact going on in a face-to-face encounter. My friend Kary wonders why he has such bad experiences at restaurants. His wife knows why. Kary always goes in with a scowl on his face, ready to fight to the death for a good table and fast, fastidious service. Think about going into the office — or a restaurant, retail establishment, or family dinner. Chances are that if you enter with a big smile on your face, people will respond with the same and seem to treat you better. It's a well-established social phenomenon.

In fact, just looking at the photos of happy-faced people has been shown to make changes in the brain. MRIs show that when a mother views photos of her own baby's face, this lights up the reward centers in the mother's brain in a way similar to that observed in studies of the brains of people addicted to drugs. The brain's reward centers also light up when mothers look at pictures of other smiling babies, though not as strongly as when the women look at their own babies.[13]

The ability to smile socially can get hammered out of us. At work, someone comes into the office and asks how the day is going, and we grimace. We don't smile, even when we need someone to help us, run out for coffee, stay late, or rerun some numbers. Check in on your snap. Notice how your smile or grimace affects others.

How to Catch a Smile

Mirror neurons help us feel what others are feeling. They are a special class of brain cells that fire not only when you make a facial expression, gesture, or move but also when you observe someone else do these things. In a snap, neurons can activate muscles to mimic those of a person you are observing. These neurons allow you to feel what she is feeling.

When you see someone smile, your tiny-as-a-grain-of-sand

mirror neurons for smiling fire up, too, re-creating in your mind the feeling associated with smiling. You don't have to think about what the other person intends by smiling; you experience the meaning immediately and effortlessly.[14]

The Magic of a Smile

Of the thirty-six muscles used to create facial expressions, the precise number of muscles used for smiling varies, depending on how researchers define a smile. We typically see a smile as a spreading and upturning of the lips. Of the muscles that produce a smile, the risorius, which pulls the corner of the mouth outward, is specific to human beings, according to Rui Diogo, a specialist in facial muscles in the anthropology department at George Washington University in Washington, D.C.[15] A smile significantly changes the face, so much so that it can be detected and recognized immediately and from a great distance — three hundred feet, or almost the length of a football field.[16]

Though they didn't attend cocktail parties where they needed to smile and make small talk, our cave-dwelling ancestors did run into other cave dwellers they did not know. So as they approached a stranger, they smiled to say, "I am harmless." Smiling is the

Personality-Type Smiles

Your smile signals some of the secrets of your personality. When I was the national spokesperson for Natural Dentist toothpaste and mouthwash, I did research on how your smile reflects your personality type. In this research, I confirmed my theory that your smile communicates which of four DISC personality types you are:

Driver: a person who likes to get things done.

Influencer: someone who especially likes to be appreciated.

Supporter: a person who likes to get along with others.

Corrector: an individual who likes to get things right.

(Go to www.snapfirst impressions.com to do the "Smile Personality" assessment. Follow the photo tutorial to learn how to identify a person's DISC type. You can also see photos of celebrities there and guess their personality types by examining their smiles.)

oldest form of expression to show a desire to cooperate. So even when the smile was three hundred feet away, cave people knew the smile connoted safety. It takes us only 0.1 millisecond to decide whether a face is happy or sad, according to researcher J. Antonio Aznar-Casanova of the University of Barcelona.[17]

Believe it or not, there are more than fifty different types of smiles. We smile not only when we are happy but also when we are experiencing many other types of feelings.

Is It a Real or Fake Smile?

To tell if someone is giving a sincere smile, look at his eyes rather than just his mouth. Look for a smile that uses the zygomatic major muscle that runs from the cheekbone down at an angle to the corner of the lips. In a "zygomatic smile," the lips turn up significantly at the corners, and the cheeks seem to lift up. This smile makes us look happy. A smile that uses just the lower part of the face is more apt to be a fake.[18]

Look for the little wrinkles at the outside corner of the eyes. Most people call them crow's-feet but I call them happy feet! Typically, when someone is really happy, his brow lowers and his eyes seem smaller. Look specifically at the muscles that surround the eye socket. A smile from joy contracts the circle of muscles around the eyes. (The muscles around the outer part of the eyes are hard to consciously control; I have found in my work and discussions with other professional observers of facial expression that only very few people, less than 10 percent of the population, can do so.)

When you're with someone who breaks into a smile, look for the wave. A real smile seems to crest over the face like a wave, changing very rapidly from a small facial movement around the lips, to lifting the sides of the face and the eyes, and then the brows, into a broad, open expression. Put your hands flat over your face right now. Let your face relax and then think of something that makes you happy — a pet, yellow daisies, chocolate ice cream. Or, simply say "money." Either way, let yourself smile. Did you feel your hands move up?

Just as with other facial expressions, *when* a smile occurs can let you know if it is heartfelt. What words and emotions accompany the smile? Typically, a person will feel happy, then smile, and then say something positive. Feel, show, say.

Research shows that we can tell from someone's voice whether she is giving a sincere smile. The voice changes when we give a real smile. Amy Drahota, a researcher in the field, says, "When we listen to speech we hear the general pitch, and people associate a rise in pitch with more smiley-sounding voices." She adds that "we might also be picking up on more subtle cues, like the spread of frequencies within the voice and how intense the voice is." The timbre of the voice accompanying a real smile is very different from that of a fake smiler. The blind have no trouble distinguishing between real and false smiles. This is why we can tell if someone is smiling when we're talking to them on the phone.[19]

Baby Smiles

Babies form the smile muscles in utero. About three weeks after birth, and probably after a good burping, babies give fleeting smiles in response to touch and sound and to visual cues like the funny faces the adults around them tend to make. Like baby Simon, mentioned earlier, babies start recognizing faces and smiling socially — that is, smiling to get you to smile and treat them well — at about eight to twelve weeks. (Just about the time you are tired of getting up at three in the morning to change diapers!)

Smiles and the Sexes

Do men and women smile differently or for different reasons? I suspect that any man who has heard his wife say, "Everything is fine," as she presses her lips together while their corners rise only slightly, knows that women fake smiles more often than men do. Fake smiles can come with a price, however. In one study, experts examined women's smiles in their yearbook photos and coded the different types of smiles they found there. Then they compared the present-day lives of the women who'd given real smiles with the lives of those who hadn't. They determined that, years later, the real smilers were leading significantly happier lives.

Men are often concerned that smiling makes them appear less powerful. This makes sense, since men with higher levels of testosterone do smile less often.[20] And although men are apt to smile less in private, they tend to be uncomfortable around women who aren't smiling.

Is there an all-American smile? Americans smile more often but are also more likely to simply part their lips and stretch the corners of their mouths to smile. Basically, we give a lot of fake smiles! Though the British have a dignified smile, they are more likely than us to smile by pulling their lips back and upward, exposing their lower teeth and giving a genuine grin. The French rarely smile at strangers — and tend to think Americans who smile all the time are nuts. But once the French know you, they smile as positively as anyone. In some cultures, people put their palms in front of their faces to cover the embarrassing show of emotion revealed by a smile. In Korea, smiling is seen as something shallow people do, while in Indonesia the resting position of the face is very often a smile. (For more cultural differences in smiling and other facial expressions, go to www.snapfirstimpressions.com.)

Everyone has a "resting face" facial expression that is on his or her face the majority of the time. Do you know what yours is like? If you have access to any videos of yourself, check it out; otherwise, seek feedback from others.

A client told me that, several times a week, total strangers asked her what was wrong. "I'm not an angry person," Sarah insisted, "but these questions are beginning to make me mad." I shared with her the important detail that her resting face did indeed look angry. We had a conversation to explore why. Turns out that Sarah was working full-time, was taking care of an elderly mother with Alzheimer's, and had a teenage daughter and a husband with health problems. She was handling all these situations with kindness and love, but just below the surface was an understandable anger that she had too much on her plate. What's more, she didn't have an outlet for expressing her frustration. But her face expressed it. As she worked to find healthy ways to express her feelings, Sarah's resting face became more restful for everyone around her. Just as the Cheshire cat in *Alice in Wonderland* left a mysterious smile in its wake, our smiles — or lack of smiles — have a lasting effect on those around us.

5. CONNECTIONS IN A SNAP

How to Match, Mirror, Listen, and Use Body Windows

While in college, I had a job doing telephone surveys for the governor's office. Yes, I was that person interrupting your dinner to ask you how many refrigerators you had, whether you owned a boat, and what you thought of the wastewater treatment in your area — you know, all those fun, stimulating topics.

I had to read from a script, with a supervisor listening in to make sure that I did so, and the surveys lasted from twenty-five minutes to an hour. I loved this job. No kidding. Most of my fellow surveyors did not. They hated it when people they called would hang up, and they hated the more-than-occasional curses they got. I wondered why they got all the mean people; my callees seemed so nice.

Soon, I was getting all the hang-ups from the other surveyors. I called the people who had slammed the phone down when called previously. I got them to complete our survey — and I got a raise. I didn't know why this was happening until I took my first nonverbal communication class at nineteen and learned about "matching and mirroring." This natural phenomenon causes you to match the body movement, voice tone, breathing, and so on of people you like. This was what I was doing without even knowing it.

If someone answered the phone with a light and happy voice, I greeted him or her with the same. If the person gave a quick, loud "Hello?" I matched it. If someone paused a lot and breathed deeply, so did I. Matching and mirroring made them feel safe and comfortable with me. At the subconscious level, they felt we were in the same "tribe." So they stayed on the phone — telling me about their refrigerators, boats, and sewage plants!

You've said hello and shaken hands — or exchanged a dap. Your eyes and smile have greeted the other person's. How does the rest of you factor into a snap?

As we saw in the last chapter, smiles can be contagious. So are other aspects of our demeanor. When someone comes into the office in a seriously bad mood, she can walk down a corridor of cubicles and, without even making eye contact, spread her mood like the flu.[1]

Isopraxism is the pull toward the energy of those around us, a tendency for animals to imitate their fellow animals' behavior. The effects of isopraxism are apparent in, for example, large groups of birds flying together in formation, fish swimming together in schools, and people in a group who yawn after they see someone else yawn. Isopraxism is what makes moods contagious. Think of the last time you caught a

> ### We Feel for You
>
> "As people nonconsciously and automatically mimic their companions' fleeting expression of emotion, they often come to *feel* pale reflections of their partners' feelings. By attending to this stream of tiny moment-to-moment reactions, people can and do 'feel themselves into' the emotional landscapes inhabited by their partners."[2]
>
> — Elaine Hatfield, John T. Cacioppo, and Richard L. Rapson, "Emotional Contagion"

fit of laughter from companions, even if you weren't sure what you were all laughing about, or a time when, in a large group, you got drawn into humor, sadness, or enthusiasm. In this phenomenon, also called emotional contagion, we feel what other people are feeling even though we may not be aware that we are "feeding" emotions to each other. (For videos demonstrating the effect, and for more information, go to "Isopraxism: Matching, Mirroring" at www.snapfirstimpressions.com.)

When I was at Florida State, we called our Saturday night football games Saturday night fever. They were exciting! Sitting close to one another, watching the same full-force body language on the field, we did catch a kind of fever. Holding my cup and hotdog, I'd see the wave coming and think, "This is lame; I'm not doing this." Then as it drew closer, I'd get pulled into the wave, as though it were a real ocean undertow — which often resulted in my cup's contents splashing up over me.

We "catch" emotions. Some researchers describe what we catch as packages of information. These packages contain many things, including others' facial, vocal, and postural expressions; conscious awareness; neurophysiological activity; autonomic nervous system activity; and instrumental behaviors.[3] We take in these information packages in ways that create empathy in us and communicate empathy to us.

Catching Someone Else's Bad Impression

When a political candidate looks at an opposing candidate with disgust, we may "catch" that disgust and, consequently, a bad impression of her opponent. In the same way, a newscaster, manager, or old friend may talk about someone not present and make a facial expression signifying disgust, and we may catch this feeling from him and form a bad impression of that person.

Mirror neurons, discussed at the end of chapter 4, allow us to catch the emotions of others. The sense of "just knowing," called "bottom-up understanding," comes from the interaction of mirror neurons that prompt our faces and bodies to do what someone else is doing. This causes us, in turn, to feel what others are feeling. "Top-down knowing" is the conscious effort to read body language and to subconsciously, or at times consciously, match others in order to understand them. The better you are at consciously interpreting body language, the more active your mirror neuron system becomes. Thus you can understand others more fully and create positive first impressions. This is the magic of the snap.

EXERCISE

Changing a Negative First Impression to a Positive First Impression

Take a minute to think of the last time you entered a room with a tense, drawn, or tired face, and sighed, whined, or complained about the weather, the traffic, your bad day, or how tired you were, or in any other way "led with your pain." Note that you may not have said anything aloud but that you may have made an impression with your facial expression of irritation, your exasperated tone of voice, and your "down" body language.

Do you do this often, sometimes, or rarely?

You wouldn't walk into a room and sneeze on someone or hand him your dirty tissue. Negative emotions are just as unpleasant, so lead with your happiness. For the next few days, before you enter a room, pause and let go of your negative emotions. Think, feel, and look positive as you enter the space. Bring your good feelings into the room to make a positive first impression.

Mirror, Mirror

Real communication — verbal and nonverbal — entails being able to see the world both through your eyes and through someone else's. Communication is about creating understanding. If you want to connect to someone in a snap, rapport is the fastest and most effective way to do so, and building good rapport is exactly what matching and mirroring do. You may have heard the term *matching* before and worried that the act of matching isn't natural, or you may have been concerned that you would do it incorrectly. Let's allay those concerns.

Rapport is a feeling of trust and safety. In a good relation, the other person feels heard and understood. When you are in rapport with another person, you have the opportunity to enter her world and see things from her perspective. The word *empathy* comes from the German word *Einfühlung*, which means "feeling into." By matching, you get the chance to literally feel the way she does and gain an understanding of exactly where she is coming from. This dramatically enhances your entire relationship.

How Does It Work?

When we hold and move our bodies in certain ways, we release specific chemicals in our brains. We are used to thinking that our demeanor reflects our feelings, but the reverse is also true: we feel and think according to the way we hold our bodies. Standing up straight and squaring and relaxing our shoulders doesn't just make us look more confident; it actually makes us *feel* this way.

Taking this one step further, when we match and mirror someone else's physiology, we get a chemical match of what's going on in her. We begin to feel what she is feeling.

Try Matching or Mirroring

While it seems like magic, it isn't, and you can do it. You are matching and mirroring all the time; it's a natural phenomenon. If you do it consciously for a moment, your body's chemical state and the other person help you produce the movement naturally. This happens very quickly; you don't have to match or mirror consciously for more than a minute.

But first, let's distinguish between mirroring and matching. Both have a positive effect. Tit-for-tat matching is a bit more subtle.

- **Mirroring** is acting as if you are a mirror of the other person. If he moves his right shoulder and leans to his left, you mirror him by moving your left shoulder and leaning to your right. If he lifts his right hand, you move your left.

- **Matching** is the reverse of mirroring. When he moves his right shoulder and leans to the left, you move your right shoulder and lean to the left. When he leans back, you lean back. When you *mirror* someone consciously, you typically mirror his movements at the same time. *Matching* is more like dancing: you wait for a beat before you match a movement. Or you may wait longer to match, perhaps until it is your turn to speak.

- **Tit-for-tat matching** is when you match the other person's movement with another type of action, sound, or movement. One person may shake his crossed foot up and down; in response, you do something else, like drum your fingers at the same pace. Or maybe he picks up a coffee cup and plays with it, and you pick up your sunglasses case and fiddle with it.

Matching and Mirroring Body Language

Body language includes facial expressions, eye movements, gestures, and postures. But start out by matching or mirroring only one behavior at a time, with one person. You can gradually, consciously match multiple body postures and movements as you get more comfortable with it. In natural matching and mirroring, you respond to hundreds of cues in milliseconds, a veritable symphony of sounds and movements. But as you learn, you may be able to play only one instrument at a time.

Matching Voice

I called my friend Pat, and her voice didn't do its typical, incredible matching. I knew that, even though she was talking to me, she really didn't have time to do so. When I checked in with her about this, she confirmed it. You've probably experienced the same thing: you're talking to someone, but something isn't quite right. Your client, friend, or sweetie isn't matching your voice or tempo.

In voice matching, you can match another person's tone (for example, it may be harsh, sarcastic, or assertive), speed (fast to slow), volume (soft to loud), rhythm (its beats and emphases), accent, clarity, or articulation (for example, how crisp or slurred the *c* and *k* sounds are). Don't match so dramatically that it sounds as if you are mocking or mimicking. Stay in a zone that's comfortable for you. For example, if someone is speaking much louder than you are, just raise your own volume a tad. You don't have to match completely or for very long. Just as I did in my telephone surveys, you can simply match for the first few moments of the interaction.

Matching Breath and Pacing

This is the trickiest thing to do well, at first, but it's powerful. You actually match the person's vocal rhythms, pauses (or lack of pauses), and breathing rate, as he speaks. I identify communicators as either "turtles" or "rabbits." Turtles are those who speak slowly and softly, pause often, and love and need silence in conversation because it gives them time to think. Rabbits, on the other hand, like loud, fast-paced communication with overlapping conversations. They hate silences. In fact, rabbits feel it their duty to fill up every moment with sound.

Turtles may think extreme rabbits are rude and overbearing. Rabbits get frustrated with extreme turtles, feeling they are slow and nonparticipatory. No one's right or wrong; both communication styles are great. The secret to a snap impression is to recognize your type and your interlocutor's type and move toward a match. Are you a turtle or a rabbit? Right now, I bet, you can name someone you recognize as the opposite of your type.

EXERCISE

Turtle or Rabbit? Slow Down or Speed Up?

As you meet three new people, or during your next three conversations, figure out where you are on the continuum between turtle and rabbit, and where on the continuum the other person is. To begin to do this consciously, it's best to be in a quiet environment so that you can focus on the other person. How quickly does she speak? When does she pause, or when does she not pause? Does she speed through a sentence and then breathe? Does she breathe deeply and slowly and then speak slowly?

When you do this well, you will almost immediately get a rush of the same feeling the other person is feeling. When done with integrity — without the desire to manipulate, and with genuine interest in the other person — this is a powerful way to connect.

Body Windows

The murder suspect sits at a table. The police are questioning him about the shotgun killing of his wife. He claims that the gun accidentally went off as he was cleaning it in the bedroom. During the interrogation, his shoulders are hunched, his chest is angled toward the door, and his hands are closed. However, when the police change the line of questioning to focus on the purchase of the gun, his arms unfold and he turns his chest toward the investigators. His chest expands and opens up as he describes how he recently decided to take up hunting, and he furnishes the details of his purchase of the guns and bullets. When the police ask him if he planned to kill his wife, he closes his body windows, picking up a soda can and pulling it close to him, covering his heart window.

Analyzing the interrogation video, I find it clear that the husband planned and rehearsed what he intended to say about purchasing the gun. However, when questions about the shooting came up, he closed his body windows to hide his guilt from the police.

When I was a child, I would sit in the grass in the backyard and play with roly-poly bugs. If I touched one, it would roll up its long body into a tight little ball to protect itself. Likewise, when we do not like or feel safe with people, we roll our bodies inward or take other actions to protect ourselves. We may bring our shoulders inward, cross our arms, zip up a jacket, or put on a pair of sunglasses. We also close our body windows when we are nervous. We may cross our legs, arms, or ankles; hide the palms of our hands; bring our heads down; or close our eyes momentarily by blinking more often.

Physical barriers and objects also offer us a way to close our windows by blocking others' view of our body. Women may hold their purses in front of their bodies; girls may place their schoolbooks in front of their chests; men may put on a tie or hold a drink at chest level. In business we hide our hearts behind our computers or put a desk between us and the salesperson whose product we don't care to buy. Businesses will put a broad, high counter or a glass window between employees and pesky customers. These actions create first impressions that send important — often negative — messages.

For example, I am clicking through the photos in the Match .com profiles of guys who have expressed interest in meeting me. After looking at thirty or forty, I spot a trend. The majority of men in my age group are standing outside next to their sports cars or their boats. Well, they are not simply standing next to them; they are facing toward them. In fact, most have their torsos and feet pointed toward their cars or boats. Yes, my potential romantic matches are dating already — they're dating their cars and boats!

My first impression is "Not *my* guy." Even though I know that their possessions (and status symbols) may make the men feel more secure about posing for photos, I am not impressed. Finally, many auto and boat photos later, I find one photo unlike all the others. It's of a smiling guy sitting with his German shepherd. His eyes are toward the camera; his heart is facing the dog. He even has his hand on the dog. It creates a warm first impression. Dog lover that I am, I know I would be happy to share him with a dog rather than a sports car. I accept this date.

So Telling, So Be Aware

As we've already seen, we have windows on many parts of our bodies: the tops of our heads, our eyes, our mouths, our throats, our upper chests or hearts, the palms of our hands, our knees, our toes, and the soles of our feet. How we open and close those windows affects our first impressions.

I began my research on what I identified as body windows in my nonverbal communication course at Florida State University when I noticed that my students, all 150 of them in one class, would open their windows when the information in class was compelling, and then they would be fully present. When it wasn't, they would place books and backpacks in front of them and turn their faces, torsos, and feet toward the exit doors that would lead them to the Florida sunshine. Their windows were closed for business.

Indeed, your body windows open and close for the three main reasons that all body language changes — because of how you are feeling about yourself, the topic, or the situation. When we like someone, we want to have our body open to that person. For instance, when you're seated in a conference room you will swivel your chair toward the person with whom you agree, and turn away from the person whose ideas you find disagreeable.

Our body windows signal to others whether we are open or closed. When we are speaking to someone with whom we feel familiar and comfortable, we may open our heart window and face him or her directly. If we have our arms uncrossed and our hands relaxed at our sides, we send the message "I am open to approach." If we cross our arms tightly, we send the message "I am closed to approach."

To be open is to allow people to make contact with you. However, you may appear too familiar if you stand or sit too close and open too much of your body to someone with whom you do not have a close relationship, or to a stranger who does not respond to your approach by opening up in kind. Notice the impression you make. Do people open or close when you approach or start a conversation? Notice how your actions, mood, and topic choices affect whether someone's windows are open or closed.

Of course, I would be remiss if I didn't mention that, just

like the windows on a house, body windows are affected by environmental factors such as temperature. Think about what happens to your body when you are physically cold. Your muscles tighten and you hold your arms tight against your chest, and your fingers tighten and close together. When you are warm, your muscles relax, you stretch out, you sit back in your chair, your legs and arms relax, and your fingers open out. It's interesting that the same body language in response to either cold or warm temperatures symbolically shows us as either cold or warm emotionally.

QUIZ

Where Would You Sit?

Where would you sit at the table in the following situations?

1. You are about to be interviewed for a job by one person, who is sitting in seat A.
2. You are selling a product or idea to one person, who is sitting in seat A.
3. You are in a social setting and want to have a great conversation with someone of your gender, who is sitting in seat A.
4. You are in a social setting and want to start a conversation with someone whom you are interested in meeting, flirting with, and dating, who is sitting in seat A.
5. You're giving a presentation, and your boss is sitting in seat B. You may stand or sit to speak from any of the other seats. All the remaining seats will be occupied by your audience.

(Answers on page 133.)

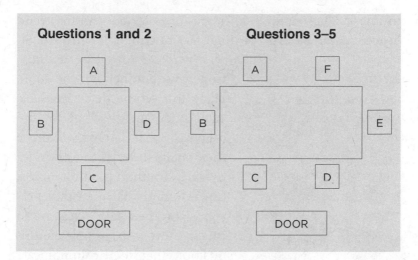

Men on the Side

One of the most powerful ways to improve your snap is to adapt the position you take when sitting or standing with someone. Though we typically think that sitting or standing face-to-face is the best way to greet and interact with someone, the real skinny is that it depends on your gender.

In personal conversation, men prefer to sit or stand side-by-side; women prefer to talk face-to-face. Men feel more comfortable and less threatened when they are not facing each other, and women feel they're more likely to be heard and understood when they do face each other.

The central body window is at the middle of the chest. I call it the heart window. When a man sits at a table, counter, or desk facing another man, and their heart windows are open, they are exposed

**Five Reasons
to Stand or Sit Side-by-Side
When Talking to Men**

1. It makes you seem friendlier.
2. It allows them to open up their body windows (see pages 134–43).
3. It makes them self-disclose, or share, more.
4. It creates more agreement between the two of you.
5. It lets you more readily establish rapport.

to attack. Their entire bodies are unprotected, and they tend to feel vulnerable. Their primal fear of danger is activated. So men who are forced to sit across from one another will be more likely to become defensive, have ego battles, and attack or criticize others. Even little boys will move their chairs in order to work side-by-side. In that position, males feel safe and that the other person is "on their side." They are so much more comfortable in this position that they communicate more openly and effectively.

See and Be Seen

Women feel they are more likely to seen by others when they sit or stand face-to-face. Their brains are wired to feel more comfortable when women are speaking in this position. Research on mother-baby bonding shows that this position allows for optimal feedback and matching. In adults, this position helps us see all body language, which aids in creating and nurturing relationships. To create the best first impression with a woman, face her as you speak.

Sitting kitty-corner at a table is a great position, because it allows you to switch easily from casual, friendly, nonconfrontational body language to a position that encourages cooperation and self-disclosure for your gender.

At one point, I was training the sales force and engineers at a large telecommunications firm to do sales presentations. Ed, an engineer, and Saul, a salesman, were preparing to give a big sales presentation to a prospect, the owner of a huge manufacturing conglomerate. Previously when they gave their pitches, Ed and Saul had sat across the table from their prospects. They'd felt the conflict that resulted from that position.

Saul wanted to create rapport and trust with this new prospective client. What would make the best snap? Saul could sit in the cooperative seat or the kitty-corner seat, and Ed could sit kitty-corner or even face-to-face with the potential client. That way Ed could answer the tough questions and Saul could be on the client's side. Ed felt confident enough to take the oppositional seat on the sales call, and all went well. They signed a million-dollar contract with the manufacturing conglomerate.

Answers to the "Where Would You Sit?" Quiz

Where would you sit at the table?

1. Custom dictates that you sit in seat C. But remember, face-to-face men may feel the need to defend themselves and compete for power. If you were being interviewed by a man, seat B would allow you to occasionally move and talk side by side, which would make the interviewer feel that you were on the same team working together.

2. Again, the traditional seat is C. C would be a great seat to take to sell to most women, who feel heard and understood when you face them. If you were selling to a man, it might be worth the small risk of not taking the traditional seat, and choosing seat B or D. You could show him your sales materials and say, "Let's look at this together," as you moved to a kitty-corner position.

3. Simply think of restaurant choices: men generally like to sit at the bar; women like to sit in a booth. If you want an easygoing conversation in a position that makes it easy for the other person to share, choose seat F if you're a man, and choose seat C if you're a woman.

4. B is a great spot, as it gives you flexibility. You can turn to the side or face the person based on how he or she responds to you. As always, you have a choice. You can choose a spot that makes you feel more comfortable or one that makes the other person feel more at ease. But it is interesting: no matter where you sit, if a woman is interested in you, she will turn to face you and/or stay facing you. To make a man feel at ease, choose seat F.

5. Because you, as the presenter, have "talking power," your boss may feel the need to compete, so he or she may interrupt to talk or ask you questions to show his or her status to the group. The traditional presenting spot E is tough, as it puts you in the "castle wall" position with the boss in the "king" spot, free to fire on you at will. If it is a

formal presentation, stand and move around the room to show your power and connection to everyone. If possible, stand between seats A and F, then move from there. If you must sit, seat A is a nice position that keeps your back away from the door, which makes you feel safer and more confident. If you have a great relationship with your boss but know of someone who is likely to disagree with you, use the gender rules: if that person is a man, sit beside him, and if that person is a woman, sit across from her.

The Different Body Windows and What They Mean

The locations of your body windows range from your feet — the most honest windows — to your knees, the center of your pelvis, your stomach, your heart, your upper chest, the front of your neck, your mouth, your eyes, and the palms of your hands. Each window opens and closes in different ways, and each sends different kinds of snap messages.

The Heart Window

The heart window is just what the name implies, a window to the heart. The heart window is located on the upper middle of the chest, which contains many vital organs, including the beating heart. Symbolically, this window reflects a person's emotional state. It is a key indicator of how we feel about ourselves and the others around us.

Try this experiment. Cross your hands and place your palms over your heart. Now think about your fears, your worries, your secrets, your anger, and your sadness. Leave your palms there for a moment, like a curtain covering your heart. Now take them down. Do you feel a little more vulnerable?

To understand the concept of the heart window, imagine that you protect this window as a knight's armor or an umpire's chest pad protects his or her chest. Now, think beyond that to something more abstract, and imagine that your window opens to the innermost part of you — your spirit, your secrets, all your dreams and fears. Consequently, when you have your window open to another, you make yourself vulnerable.

We open and close our heart window in four ways: through the clothing we wear, the way we position our heart window toward or away from someone, the use of physical barriers such as books and counters, and through our arm and shoulder placement.

The heart window is one of the most significant parts of the body because it reveals someone's true feelings. In order to understand the significance of this window, let's look at how we use barriers to close it.

Clothing can open the window to the heart or cover it like a curtain. Imagine the difference between a woman in a low-cut sweater and one wearing a high-neck blouse. Imagine a reality star from the Jersey Shore wearing a buttoned-up Oxford shirt instead of the open-to-the-waist shirt that bares his chest. Can you see the president come out for the State of the Union address wearing a tank top? Hiding or revealing the heart window with high- or low-neck clothing gives an impression of a person as tight or loose, reserved or wild, ready for and all about business or ready for a personal, relaxed, all-for-fun interaction.

The Belly Window

I am doubled over with laughter watching comedian Wanda Sykes talk about Esther, the name she's given to the fat rolls on her tummy. Esther calls out to her to "pull into the Cheesecake Factory" and later demands to be freed from her Spanx, the form-flattering underwear that Wanda wore to make a good first impression on an evening talk show.

Whether we call it the stomach, the gut, the paunch, the ventral area, or (since fat rolls are part of the window and may affect whether you are comfortable having it open or closed) by my favorite name, Esther, the belly window is that oh-so-sensitive-to-injury, sucked-in gut we see when we stand in front of a mirror. The belly window is the area between the bottom of the ribs and the top of the hips. This area is particularly vulnerable to attack. It is the area that is often punched or stabbed in a fight. Holding our hands across our bellies can be a defensive act when we fear any form of physical or emotional attack. Notice when people cover or touch their stomachs. Ask yourself what you can do or say to make them more comfortable.

Because of the chest-waist-hips "perfect" body ratio, we consider a flat tummy desirable. It indicates fitness and health in both women and men. We know that this body ratio is desirable, and we know it requires effort and/or discomfort. That's why you see men use their muscles to pull in the belly when a cute girl walks by, and why women wear Spanx. Years ago, the book and movie *Waiting to Exhale* expressed women's desire to be able to relax from the effort of looking good for men. Men and women both find that "letting it all hang out" may be great on the couch but not so great for business meetings. When we feel uncomfortably close to someone, we may pull our vulnerable upper body and head away in a situation and thus stick out the tummy to counterbalance the movement.

Rubbing or Holding the Belly Window

The belly area contains the stomach and the intestine, both of which are used to process food. When we overeat, or when something we eat or drink disagrees with us, that area may be subject to assorted pains. Rubbing the stomach can mean a person has a digestive problem or tummy ache. The abdominal walls contain significant muscles, and we can carry tension here. Rubbing, holding, or covering the belly window can also indicate tension from excessive worry.

The Neck Window

The neck window is the window of ego and communication. Did you ever wonder why, even after all these years of casual dress, men still wear an incredibly expensive piece of cloth tied around the neck in a knot? From an objective standpoint, it seems ridiculous. But a tie is a designer curtain covering up the heart window. The tie is worn only in formal work or social situations. It indicates the seriousness of the business at hand and shows the wearer's status. What do men who wear ties do when they leave work and go home or go out with friends? They loosen up or take off their ties, opening their heart and neck windows.

The reason men wear something so uncomfortable is that it's a symbol of business formality. In the early 1980s, when women were making inroads into management positions in the workplace, they began to wear big, wide bows at the necks of their blouses. Then in the mid-80s, they wore big scarves that covered their hearts. They needed to show they were serious about taking on the workplace, and they needed the bows and scarves to protect their heart windows — like a knight's armor. These bows and scarves physically and symbolically covered up and protected their sexuality.

The Self Window

Between the heart and neck windows is the self window. Take the fingertips of your right hand and place them on this part of your upper chest, at the sternum, or breastbone. Behind the sternum is the thymus gland, which regulates the immune system and is where T cells mature. This is a body language location that has been studied as part of many religions and spiritual practices. In metaphysics, this spot is called the higher heart chakra, or "I am" point. It makes sense that when someone wants to "disappear" because of fear, surprise, or embarrassment he may use his hand or fingertips to cover the self window. And it is interesting to note that when you raise your hands in prayer, you place your hands over the heart, neck, and self windows.

People often subconsciously touch the part of the sternum that rests over the thymus gland when they are stressed. Notice when you cover, touch, or rub this area. Ask yourself what about the other person or people, situation, or topic is stressful and what you can do to make yourself and others more comfortable.

Upper-Body Signals

The upper body includes shoulders, arms, and hands. Though we are focusing on windows, remember that parts of the body can give you insights but that you must read the entire body, what is called a "gesture cluster," to get the full message.

The shoulders and arms are among the most visible parts of the body in many instances. They can normally be seen across a desk, above a countertop, and on the other side of a table. During a conversation, our gaze focuses most often on the triangle formed by the eyes and mouth, but we do spend a significant time studying the upper torso for information.

Symbolically, the shoulders and the arms surround and extend out of the heart. Because these body parts come out from the heart, we can see the arms and hands as expressions of what's in the heart. Arm and hand movements are the body's clearest emotional barometers. The shoulders, arms, and hands are also considered the "doers" of the body. Notice whether people reach out and move toward you to connect or pull back and retreat. A soft spot at the crook of each arm is a window to our vulnerability, and we have windows at the palms of the hands.

If a person wants to hide what he is doing or has done, or wants to hide his emotional state, he will close the windows at the palms of the hands by hiding them. The most frequently asked question by participants in my public speaking classes is "What can I do with my hands?" They long to have their hands hidden because hands reveal the speaker's emotional state. A person may cover or touch the inside of her elbow when she is nervous or feeling emotionally intruded upon and not comfortable about saying so out loud.

The shoulders are the base for the head, and the link to the emotional outlet of the hands and arms. If you examine the male and female silhouettes, you'll see that males tend to have large, broad shoulders and women have small, narrow shoulders. As women took on men's jobs during World War II, shoulder pads became popular in women's clothing. The female silhouette symbolically indicated its ability to carry the weight of work while men were away at war. When women began to take on a greater number of management positions in the 1980s, shoulder pads came back into style. Just like the powerful actresses of the forties — Joan Crawford, Barbara Stanwyck, and Bette Davis — the powerful women on daytime television, and on nighttime soaps such as *Dynasty*, wore shoulder pads as if to say, "I can be as strong and mighty as a man." In the nineties the female clothing style of bulky, oversized shirts and sweaters worn with skinny jeans or leggings created the silhouette of a short but broad-shouldered man. Now big tops and wide belts are worn with leggings and high heels and tall boots. We've grown.

Hand It Over

In teaching interview and interrogation techniques, I ask law enforcement officers to study the palms of the people they question. It is difficult for people to lie with the palms of their hands exposed. Liars tend to keep their hands hidden and still. They stick them in their pockets, clench them, or hold them behind their backs. I tell the officers to imagine that the person they suspect of lying holds the truth in the palms of her hands, and to see if she'll show it to them.

The phrase "you seem to be carrying the weight of the world on your shoulders" is often said of round-shouldered people. People who seem to take on the burdens of life, or more responsibilities than they can possibly handle, round their shoulders and bend forward from the accumulated weight. As you take your snaps, notice that people's shoulders may lower when they feel judged or criticized and that the shoulders may pull back and the head and chest may rise in "up" body language when they feel praised and respected. Some older people stoop because of osteoporosis or lack of exercise. I have scoliosis, a curvature of the spine that causes a stoop-shouldered look. One of the reasons I am so drawn to body language is that I have learned that my large gestures and animation help to overcome the negative image produced by my stooped posture.

Shoulders may also tell a story about abuse. I can walk into a room to give a speech and tell immediately which audience members have suffered long years of abuse. People who have been abused will draw their shoulders together to protect their hearts, closing their heart windows. If that habit continues, it affects the posture, so you can look at someone's habitual posture and see evidence of a broken heart or even a current abusive relationship. Young girls may draw their shoulders forward because they are self-conscious about their breasts and wish to shield them from view. This roly-poly body posture is a key gesture cluster I share when I teach foster parents how to recognize whether children brought into their homes have suffered physical or sexual abuse. Therapists say that one of the most accurate indicators that a client had an overbearing father, or was or is in an abusive relationship, is bowed or hunched shoulders.

As the saying goes, for the turtle to get anywhere it has to stick its neck out. The turtle hides by pulling its head into its shell. When we stand up straight with our shoulders back, we present a strong front. When we raise our shoulders up toward our ears in a shrug, we create a turtle-like effect, lowering and protecting our head, retreating into our shell, or symbolically distancing ourselves from a situation we don't want or don't know how to handle. Often you will see a shoulder shrug combined with a head tilt and open palms. This combination signals "I'm helpless."

EXERCISE

See for Yourself

Think about your own body and how you hold your shoulders. Stand with your back against a wall in your normal relaxed posture. Do your shoulders press against the wall?

Stand and then sit in front of a full-length mirror and examine your posture. What do you see? What silhouette are you showing to the world? What do you think it means? Do you think it has changed or can change? How do others respond to you? Shrug your shoulders. How do you look?

Monitor your posture and upper-body windows, and see how they affect your mood and others' impressions of you. Be sure to ask your friends and colleagues for feedback so you can understand the impression you're making.

Find some photos of yourself in different kinds of clothes — casual and dressy. How do different outfits affect your posture and the impression you give others?

Lower-Body Windows: The Knees and Feet

When we read body language, we read from the feet to the top of the head, because the most honest portion of the body is from the waist down. When we feel safe, comfortable, and relaxed, we tend to have our windows open. We typically only close down when we are tense or fearful. And since we are often socialized not to show our nervousness, those cues to nervousness, tenseness, or fearfulness will often "leak out" through the feet.

Imagine you are talking to a man whose upper body is aimed toward you but whose legs and feet are turned toward the exit. He may be indicating that he wants to leave. When you notice this, you should consider the topic you are discussing and how the person feels about you. Then ask yourself if he is nervous and saying with his body, "I really want to be out of here." If he jiggles or taps a foot, especially toward an exit, he is symbolically running away or is nervous. What can you do to make the conversation comfortable?

A "foot lock," in which one foot wraps around the leg, usually at the lower calf, is like having a "closed" sign hanging on the door. The person may be sitting with the rest of her body open, but the foot lock shows her true feelings. People who are relaxed will tend to take up more space with their legs. This is especially true when men stand with their feet far apart or sit with their legs apart; they are signaling that they are relaxed and confident.

The bottom of the foot also has a window. A reporter from India was interviewing me at my house when she noticed my little shoe case near the door. "Do you take off your shoes when you enter your house?" she asked me.

"Yes," I replied. "I love going barefoot indoors, and it keeps dirt from being tracked into the house."

She began to tell me about the custom in some parts of India of leaving your shoes by the door and putting on slippers to walk into the house. She said that the streets of cities like Mumbai are very dirty, and that houses are holy places, so people there want to leave the filth of the street outside of the home.

I talked about the symbolism of the window at the bottom of the foot and said that in American culture, men often cross their legs, which shows the bottom of the foot to the person or people they are with. The symbolism says, "I am so powerful and strong, I could step on you if I wanted to." I asked about the Indian cultural taboo against showing the bottom of the foot. I had told my audiences for years that this foot posture was seen in Indian culture as extremely insulting, but I had never known why. She told me that because the streets are filthy, showing the bottom of your foot is like saying, "You are like the filth on my feet; I have no respect for you." What a great insight. This posture is also considered rude in many other countries, and by those of the Muslim faith. It is such a simple posture, yet imbued with so much power.

I teach a class called Meeting of the Minds. As the title suggests, we get into some heated discussions concerning what most people feel are hot topics, like religion, sex, and politics. For the past nine years, I have noticed that the more potent debates start with everyone seated and their legs uncrossed, chairs pulled up to the discussion table, and bodies bent over and leaning toward the other people at the table. I watch closely as a controversial topic is introduced. Then I often see one person push away from the table, lean back, and cross his legs or turn his feet away from the speaker. Immediately, I can identify the dissident thinker in that group. The next time you are in a heated discussion, watch closely.

Think about this the next time you are sitting at a meeting. Just because you're not saying anything out loud to the speaker about the content, your body windows may be speaking volumes.

Crossing Over:
Different Arm Crosses and What They Mean

I was brought into a corporate meeting to observe the nonverbal communication of the most senior executives in the organization, including the CEO, CFO, and CIO and general managers, and to coach these leaders in nonverbal communication and in presentation.

I looked around the room after a break and noticed that, as these people came back into the room and sat down, they all opened their throat, stomach, and heart windows to the president. I thought, "This is great." The chairman then brought everybody to attention by announcing a change in the agenda: the new CFO was going to present the annual reports of each division. Immediately, before the CFO even started talking, I noticed several key people touch their stomachs and/or cross their arms. As the CFO began to talk about certain divisions, I saw the managers and team members in those divisions cross their arms and close other body windows.

When the CFO asked for questions, he was met with total silence. When he asked what the others thought of the information, there was more silence.

Here is the irony: After the meeting, I worked individually with the team members. Nobody from that audience remembered anything that was said; they just thought the CFO was "boring." They hadn't picked up on how they'd closed down when he talked about them. When I worked with the CFO, he began by saying he thought he did a great job on the speech because no one interrupted or asked questions.

You don't have to be talking about financial figures or employee performance to provoke crossed arms. My friends love to introduce me as a body language expert. And no matter who I am introduced to, the person inevitably crosses his or her arms, gives a tight downward smile, steps away from me, and then says, "Nice to meet you."

There are dozens of interpretations for an arm cross. In my work, I have labeled over fifty different arm crosses, each with its own specific snap. Here are the most common arm crosses:

Quick cross: In the quick cross, the arm goes across the front of the person's body and protects the thorax (heart and lungs) and the ventral area (belly). This movement covers the person's nervousness because she seems to be doing something else. She may be adjusting her shirt cuff, watchband, button, or collar, or checking a cell phone or other device. I often see a quick cross in celebrities about to give an apology statement. The arm cross in front of the body is like a shield.

Fist cross: In this one, the arms are crossed and the hands are made into fists. This is a strong sign of *hostility* as well as *defensiveness*. If the fist cross is combined with a tight-lipped smile or clenched teeth and red face, a verbal or even physical attack could happen. A conciliatory approach is needed to discover what is causing this posture if the reason is not apparent.

Wrist cross: One arm crosses the other, forming an X at the wrist, with arms relaxed. The person may be bored or not fully engaged.

Elbow-out cross: The elbows point forward, acting as symbolic weapons that the person wants to fire at you. This can indicate that your listener is angry or disagrees with what you are saying.

Thumbs-up, too-cool-for-school arm cross: This posture says the person is defensive, but superior. It is seen in situations where someone wants to look cool and in control while still maintaining a level of protection behind his crossed arms. I have seen so many gangster rappers in this pose in their videos that I think it must be a part of a gangster training video!

Friendly Skies?

When preparing to teach presentation skills to the Federal Aviation Administration, I observed a meeting between the agency and neighborhood residents who would be affected by a new runway and flight path for the Atlanta airport. When the meeting started, twenty-one of more than a hundred residents had their arms crossed in some manner. When the FAA official began speaking, more people crossed their arms. As they did, the FAA official's speech got faster and louder as he pushed to get through the "wall" of crossed arms.

I have seen this thousands of times as a presentation coach. When speakers feel stressed or as if their audience has shut down, they go faster. Some speakers get louder and more aggressive, while some get more anxious and apologetic, but they all tend to rush. Whenever you feel like people aren't paying attention or are distracted or closed off, try slowing down or asking a question.

By the end of the FAA presentation, only three people in the audience didn't have their arms crossed. All three were from the FAA. It wasn't surprising, but when the first residents got up to speak, all but seven people's arms came uncrossed in the group of residents, and all four FAA people crossed their arms!

Muscle-hug cross: Crossing the arms and grabbing the biceps or elbows is the muscle-hug cross. It says the person wishes his muscles were bigger. This person is fearful and insecure. He is not able to fight you now — but he wishes he could.

Partial-arm cross: One arm swings across the body to hold or touch the other arm to form the barrier in a one-arm hug. Partial arm barriers are often seen in meetings where the person may be a stranger to the group or lacks self-confidence.

Broken-zipper cross: This one is also called the fig leaf. The hand is protecting the center of the pelvis. Needless to say, we protect vulnerable parts of the body. This is typically a male gesture. Children may use this gesture when they are being admonished. I see it in humble homeless men in lines outside the Atlanta soup kitchen and in executives when their bosses enter the room.

People often tell me they don't cross their arms to close people out but do it because it feels comfortable. There are two reasons they may feel more comfortable with arms crossed. First, crossing your arms can make you feel warmer. Here's why: science tells us that the freeze-flight-fight-or-faint survival response begins with specialized nerve cells in the hypothalamus. A cascade of chemical signals and nerve impulses results in a rush of adrenaline, which prepares the body for exertion. The blood is channeled away from the skin to the large muscles of the limbs (as well as to the vital organs, so our heart beats faster and our lungs take in more oxygen). Without the blood to warm the surface of the skin, we feel cooler. So guess what? We often cross our arms to get warm because we are stressed. Second, the brain is wired to feel that if we cover the heart, we will protect it from harm.

(For more arm-cross interpretations, with photos, go to "Arm Cross Interpretations" at www.snapfirstimpressions.com.)

We Need Our Space

In many cultures the sense of self — what you consider to be part of you and your space — extends past the physical body and into an intimate so-called zone of space. This was determined by anthropologist Edward T. Hall, one of the fathers of nonverbal communication, who first published his theory in the 1950s. When I took my first college course in body language and nonverbal communication in the 1970s, Hall's classic work on the personal and territorial spaces that he labeled zone parameters was still being quoted as the definitive research. We nonverbal-communication researchers continue to use those zone names, but I have seen the parameters of each zone change a bit over the years. My definitions for the zones below represent a mixture of findings in the published research and my own research and observations in public, private, and business settings.

Intimate zone: Zero to eighteen inches. Back in the 1950s we let people get closer to us. The outer boundary of this zone was just fourteen inches. When people are within arm's reach or closer, we can touch them. We can also see more detail in their body language and look them in the eye. At this range, other people are blotted out. Romance of all kinds happens in this space. Entering the intimate zone without an invitation, however, can be seen as a threat; people who approach too close are saying they invade your turf at will.

Personal zone: At one and a half to four feet apart, people are more direct in their conversations than they are when standing farther apart. This is the ideal distance for two people talking in earnest about something. If you get closer than this, you can't see the full body from the toes to the top of the head. This is also the distance people seem to maintain while standing in clusters. In chapter 9 I discuss how to enter this space easily.

Social zone: Within the two-to-four-foot social zone, we feel a connection with others that we don't feel when standing farther apart. When people are closer, we can talk without having to shout but can still keep them at a safe distance. This is the comfort zone for people standing in a group or gathered in a room.

Professional zone: This used to measure four to seven feet, about the distance between the heads of two people if one is sitting at a traditional office desk and the other is seated in a visitor's chair on the opposite side and facing him. Now this zone expands and contracts depending on the business environment or cultural rules. Cubicles mean we work closer to one another, but we seem to want more space between ourselves and others when we're given a choice of where to stand or sit. When we are using technology, such as phones and computers, we can work more closely with one another. And if we are using a device and someone else isn't, we may be oblivious to the other person's body-bubble walls.

Public zone: This is generally a space that measures fifteen feet between one person and another. To feel completely safe and at ease, we try to keep this much space between ourselves and others. But unless you live in a very sparsely populated town, this isn't always possible.

When others step within this radius, we begin to look at them more carefully. The closer they get to us, the more we become ready for appropriate action. With greater distance comes a sense of safety. If another person does something threatening, we have time to dodge, run, or prepare for battle. With less distance — in, say, a crowded airport or shopping center — we remain tense. Concerning your snap impression, know that people begin assessing you at fifteen feet. If you're going for a job interview or on your first Match .com date, this is where the comparison between the résumé or online profile and reality begins.

Rules about social distance vary with different groups of people. You can detect this by watching others for reactions. Do they step back or to the side? Do they close their body windows? People who live in crowded cities, for example, are used to closer quarters than those who live in wide-open spaces. The latter may keep extra space around themselves even in social settings.

People in other countries also view social space differently. Watch a Japanese or Chinese person talking at a party with someone from rural North America. Chances are good that you'll see the Asian person step forward and the westerner step back.

Gentler Listening

You're sitting in the office with a prospective client or customer as she talks about her needs or problems. You want her to know you're listening. You know it's important to show concern, but you're a little tired and preoccupied. Perhaps she's going on and on, or maybe she's saying some negative things and you're feeling a little defensive. What can you do to focus, increase your attention, and let the speaker know you are listening?

Most of us have far more training in reading, writing, and speaking than we do in listening, even though all of us spend far more time listening. A study by Carolyn Coakley and Andrew Wolvin in 1991 found that most experts agree that people spend about 9 percent of waking hours writing, 15 percent reading, 30 percent speaking, and 45 percent listening. Among executives, time spent listening is even higher — 55 percent or more on average.[4] Business survey results rank listening among the top three skills needed in employees, managers, and new hires. Hundreds of studies show the importance of listening in business and personal success. What nonverbal cues show that you are listening?

My fifth-grade teacher, Mrs. Arnow, taught me and my classmates a lot about listening and first impressions. She would talk to us before we went into the cafeteria, played with another class for the first time, or went on field trips. I can see her standing in one of her big, flowered dresses and hear her strong Southern-accented voice saying, "You may meet someone new; be a *gentle*man or *gentle*woman. Be polite, pay attention, and listen." In order to establish a good first impression, you need to follow Mrs. Arnow's advice and be "gentler" with your listening.

> ### Gentler Listening Tip Sheet
> **G**ive facial feedback.
> **E**ye contact: use as much as possible when conversing.
> **N**od your head to acknowledge that you hear what the speaker is saying.
> **T**urn off electronics and give your full attention to the speaker.
> **L**ean forward to show physical interest.
> **E**xpose your heart and turn the upper body toward the speaker.
> **R**emove barriers that stand in the way and block you from getting the speaker's message.

Remember that likability, our second first-impression factor, is affected by the empathy we show others. To show you're empathetic, be gentler. Each letter in the word *gentler* can remind you of how to show that you're listening, as demonstrated in the following discussion. (Bear with me as I repeat myself a bit here. I revisit these basics because they're so important in your snap.)

Give facial feedback: It is so easy to zone out as a listener. When you do, you can give a blank, open-mouthed look that resembles the face of a kid after five hours of cartoons. You're not winning friends and influencing people that way.

You may think it's not a good idea to have an expressive face and reveal your emotions, but it is a big deal and it *is* a good idea. As you'll recall, people with expressive faces are better liked and more popular. When we know someone's honest responses, we feel more comfortable around them, we can predict their behavior, and we can trust them. As you listen and your face shows your feelings about what you're hearing, the listener can also get information about where to go with what he is saying. If you look disinterested, he can get more animated. If you look puzzled, he can give more details.

You have to work your abs to have toned stomach muscles, and you have to work your face to have toned empathy skills. Let your facial expressions show your emotional response to the speaker's message. If he is concerned, show understanding by furrowing your brow. If he is unhappy, frown and lower your eyes. If he is angry, close and flatten out your lips like a sealed envelope. Briefly matching his facial expressions not only shows you are listening but also, as we've seen, creates the same chemicals in your brain that he is experiencing, so that you feel what he is feeling and you understand him better.

Eye contact: The listener should make eye contact more often than the speaker does. Recall that if you want to have good rapport, you should maintain eye contact 60 to 70 percent of the time when someone is speaking to you. Research shows that females are better at this than males and actually need more eye contact from listeners to feel comfortable in the conversation. Men tend to make little or no eye contact with those they talk to, perhaps because they do not need as much eye contact. This may explain why men can say they are listening when they are sitting with their eyes riveted on the TV screen. This gender difference in eye-contact needs shows up at an early age. Research on small children shows that little boys told to converse on a topic sat side-by-side and talked to each other while staring off into space. Little girls moved their chairs to face each other and watched each other with full attention during their entire conversation. Gender hardwiring is no excuse, however; look when you're listening.

Nod your head: You do not have to be a bobble-head toy, just occasionally nod your head to show you are listening and empathizing. An added bonus of nodding your head is that it releases endorphin-like chemicals into your bloodstream to make you feel good and feel more affable about the speaker. Be aware that women nod their heads whether they agree with the speaker's message or not. Men may think that you agree with them if you nod too much, so be careful not to give perfunctory "I'm listening" nods if you disagree with what a man is saying.

Turn off electronics: Tom brought his three-year-old, Sam, to his first meeting with a prospective client, saying, "I am so busy, I had to bring my son." Little Sam was adorable, and Tom was clearly proud of him. Little Sam kept wanting Tom's attention — asking him to play, making noise, and interrupting the conversation. Tom turned away from his client several times to take care of little Sam, even leaving the table to take Sam for milk and cookies. The client was clearly frustrated but didn't know the polite way of handling the situation with someone he had just met.

Read this story again, replacing the words little Sam with smartphone and cookies and milk with important call or text. The energy and attention we give to our electronics is like the constant caretaking of a toddler. Fellow mothers may forgive your attention to a real toddler, but clients, coworkers, and friends may wonder how present you are, how smart you are, and how much you care about them if you spend too much time coddling your electronic devices.

We carry our smartphones and other electronic devices with us in order to communicate with people who are not physically with us. We may not realize that those same devices create a barrier to communicating with the people who are right in front of us. We have become so accustomed to checking our texts and emails and answering the phone as we talk face-to-face with people that we may have forgotten what a real listener looks like. Even when someone comes into our office, our eyes may wander to the computer screen and our hands may not leave the keyboard.

Turn off the electronics and put them away. Don't use the excuse "Everybody else is doing it." Instead, create a ritual of engagement. Signal your intent to listen by turning away from your computer in the office. If you have an electronic device, take it out and say aloud, "Let me turn this off and put it away while we talk." It's amazing what a difference it will make in the snap impression you give the person you are listening to.

Lean forward: Proximity — being *physically close* — signals your desire to be emotionally or physiologically close. I don't mean you should get in someone's face, but merely lean in toward the speaker. Research shows that in a seated conversation, leaning backward communicates that you are dominant. A forward lean shows interest. Of course, if the conversation is a long one you shouldn't spend the whole time at the edge of your seat; you can vary your leaning depending on what is being said.

Expose your heart: You do not need to unbutton your shirt and show your Superman *S* to show you're listening; just make sure you turn toward the speaker. Orient the heart and, ideally, the upper portion of your body toward her. People self-disclose more to listeners who face them. Even a quarter turn away signals a lack of interest to the speaker and makes the speaker shut down. It also says something about your response to the message.

As noted earlier, research shows that when people feel under attack and/or defensive, or have low self-esteem, they protect their vulnerable heart area. To communicate that you are an open, confident speaker and listener, you need to show your heart. However, remember that there are gender differences in this regard. If you want two of your male employees or coworkers to resolve an issue or form a plan together, seat them side-by-side rather than across from each other.

Remove barriers: This means you must take away things that block your access to or view of the speaker. The barrier used most often is folded arms. Though we've seen that there are many motivations for folding our arms, speakers see any arm folding as a barrier and a cue that you are not listening. In fact, of all the different body language postures, the arm fold is the most obvious indication of a lack of interest. We actually reduce our ability to listen by crossing our arms. In a study I researched in grad school, subjects who were asked to listen to a lecture with arms folded across their chests, and then quizzed on its contents, actually retained 38 percent less information than a control group did. Those subjects also had a more negative view of the speaker and higher levels of stress.

Can Open Arms Help You Retain Knowledge?

For eleven years when I taught college, I replicated a study I did on arm folding in graduate school, and I have replicated it with audiences in hundreds of different corporate settings. It is amazing how much the arm cross cuts down on people's retention of information. In some of my informal surveys, half the audience members who did not fold their arms received scores of one hundred percent on their tests, and those who folded their arms got all twenty questions wrong. It is also interesting how quickly audience members who fold their arms lose interest.

Holding a beverage in front of your upper chest is another way to show you are blocking a speaker's message. So unfold your arms and move the phone, computer, books, or any stacks of papers on the desk that sit between the front of your body and the speaker.

Your Obligation as a Listener

When I was in graduate school, I studied with one of the world's foremost authorities on listening, Dr. Larry Barker. Dr. Barker, who was then president of the International Listening Association, wrote the first college textbook on listening ever published, and the second college textbook on body language. While working with him, I studied research on the effect of the listener's body language on the speaker. It fascinated me so much that I replicated the study as part of my master's program. The research showed that the more listening cues the listener gave, and the more animated she was, the more animated the speaker became. The speaker spoke with more energy, picked up his pace, and gestured more. The fewer cues the listener gave, the less animated and more stilted the speaker became; his voice slowed down and became a soft monotone. Many speakers even stopped gesturing altogether. In any conversation, it is your responsibility as listener to inspire and energize the speaker with your feedback.

Remember, there is no greater gift to give to others than to understand them, to really see them and give them your interest. Be "gentler" with your listening.

6. YOUR TECHNO IMPRESSION

Impress Others by Phone, Email, Facebook, Twitter, Other Social Media, and Gadgets

A client of mine met a new business partner for lunch. He told me, "We had been talking on the phone and texting for months, but I hadn't met him face-to-face." My client continued, "Five minutes after we sit down for lunch, my new partner is checking his smartphone for messages from the guy he'd just had his real lunch with. He apologizes for eating before our lunch, saying he would have dessert with me. He continues to check messages and texts throughout lunch, his head down and fingers flying. I am floored because, when I met him on the phone, I thought he was a brilliant, busy guy. I guess he is so brilliant that his mind needs to be occupied at all times. But in person, he comes off like a techno jerk."

I bet you've had a similar experience. It's easy to be critical of how others use their technology, and for high-tech users to have a poor impression of low-tech users. How is technology affecting your interactions, and how is the way you use technology influencing what people think of you?

A techno impression, or *technic*, is the impression you give others when you communicate with them by phone, email, Facebook, Twitter, or other social media, as well as when you interact with your gadgets while in the presence of other people. Once upon a time, people made the most of first impressions by meeting face-to-face. Now we don't meet face-to-face because we all have our heads down, gazing at our devices. People don't have their hearts open; they have their laptops open. They don't shake hands; they flip their handheld devices open to check for messages. They don't lean toward their seatmates to say hello; they pull out their cell phones to take a call. They are not connecting with the other people in the room, because they are communicating via a little device to someone somewhere else. *Technic* is our new communication mode. We need to get excited about it and create the most effective ways to use it.

We live in a digital world. The numbers are staggering: 80 percent of people in North America have some kind of portable phone and/or tablet. Nearly one out of every ten people on the planet uses Facebook, and the site handles 1.7 billion interactions *a minute*. Almost one million new people sign up for Facebook every single day. In 2010, the number of users passed 500 million. *Fast Company* blogger Steven Rosenbaum writes, "By 2014, the technology research group Gartner predicts social networking services will replace email as the principal method of interpersonal communications for 20% of business users."[1]

The Radicati Group, which provides research on messaging and collaboration, estimates the number of emails sent per day (in 2010) to be around 294 billion, with the average professional receiving between 80 and 150 emails each day.[2] We are communicating in a totally new way through email, texting, blogging, YouTube, video calls, web meetings, and virtual worlds. There are ever more people to "talk" to, more people to text and video call. We now have the technology to implant electronic communication devices in our brains. We can also put contacts with built-in screens on our eyes and tattoo computers on our wrists. (For details on this and other ways we are changing how we communicate using technology, go to "Techno Impressions" at www.snapfirstimpressions.com.)

All this means that we are almost constantly sending and receiving first impressions. We have to adjust, and to create new ways of managing snap impressions as technology continues to explode. My clients hire me to train their employees in the newest and best *technic* behavior. Based on the latest research, my experience with my clients, and just plain common courtesy, the guidelines I give you in this chapter will allow you to make a good impression in this brave new world.

Let's start by understanding why so many of us have difficulty turning off our electronic devices and interacting face-to-face.

When you talk to other people in person, you lay down neural pathways to the social centers of your brain. The more you interact interpersonally, human to human, the stronger the pathways become. Meeting people and talking to them becomes easier and you become more skilled and confident at making a great first impression.

Our Brains on Tech

When you interact with a technological device, you make quick, shallow decisions. You accept or don't accept a text, an invitation to click on a web link, an incoming call, and so on. These rapid decisions lay down pathways to the ego centers of your brain. In fact, doing so gives you a bit of a high and makes you feel superior to those around you. You can now understand the techno jerk who seems irritated and uncomfortable when he has to stop and talk to you. Unfortunately, to successfully make quick, shallow decisions, you have to weaken pathways to the social centers of your brain. You're laying down tracks to the ego center that produces that nice addictive high, but interpersonal communication becomes more difficult — and may even feel like an inferior means of interacting.

The constant checking, looking for more information, not fully focusing on anything or anyone, puts our brains in a heightened state of stress. Our "continuous partial attention," a term coined by software executive Linda Stone in the 1990s,[3] means that techno connecting is keeping us high because we are always on red alert, always searching for a new contact or exciting news, trying to stay one tidbit of trivia up on the next guy. Once we get used to it, we thrive on the perpetual high of connectivity. We are surfing the Internet, riding the big kahuna wave, and this feeds our ego. The rush is irresistible.[4] Eventually, however, our hypothalamus overloads, and we wipe out.

Technology is here and it is reshaping our brains. We need to change the way we interact to reduce our stress and give ourselves the best relationships possible.

The Four Rules of Techno Impressions: How to Use Devices in the Presence of Real Live People

"There's a whole nation of people out there looking down. Are they depressed? Scanning for change? Seeing if they're still slim enough to see their shoes?"[5] This is comic Anna T. Collins's description of the world of people staring down at their electronic devices. Yes, many of us are now spending much of our waking time with heads down, hunched over some bit of technological wizardry.

When it comes to texting, phone calls, and all the other interactions you have with portable devices, you have to think about the impression you are making on those who are in your physical presence, and not just on those you are communicating with.

Rule 1. When in Doubt, Turn It Off and Put It Away

Now you know why this is hard to do; we are literally addicted to our devices, and they make us feel good temporarily. But they make us look "stuck-up" too, and they can eventually take away our ability to carry on a conversation face-to-face. Tech devices distract us, entertain us, and keep us company. We form a bond with them. But think of any electronic device as a three-year-old child and ask yourself, "Would I have my three-year-old at the table with me while talking to this person?"

Rule 2. Create a Formal Turn-Off-Technology Ritual, Just as You Have a Formal Handshake Greeting

When you sit down with someone face-to-face, take out any device you have, turn it off, and put it out of your line of sight. You can even say out loud, "I am turning this off and putting it away because you and our meeting are important."

When your devices are sitting in front of you, they create a physical barrier between you and the other person. Research shows that they also create an emotional barrier, because even if they're sitting there quietly, their presence implies that they are as important as your human partner or more so.

> **Prioritize**
>
> I suggested the "I'm turning this off and putting it away" ritual to a client (Deloitte, the world's largest management consulting firm). They were intrigued, not just by the idea of putting devices away, but also by the notion of informing the people you are with that you've done so. It's such a simple act, but it powerfully conveys a sense of respect and attention. The firm wanted to make it a company-wide recommendation.

Rule 3. Keep It Down in Public Places

Your cell phone calls should be brief and at a low volume. And the content of your conversation should be rated "G" for general public suitability.

Too Much Information

At your favorite restaurant, you decide to break with your usual routine and have a drink in the bar before eating. You're thinking it would be nice to meet someone new, someone else who likes the restaurant's friendly atmosphere. Your smartphone vibrates as you sit on a stool, and you see that it's a good friend calling, so you take the call. The bar is a little loud, and your friend too is out and about, so you raise your voice. Your friend is telling you a funny story about her bad blind date the previous night, and before you know it you're laughing and gesturing. As you drain your pinot grigio, you share a blind date story of your own, complete with an R-rated detail or two. Your friend tells you she can't hear you, so you raise your voice a bit more. As you do, you notice the bartender shaking his head at you — and a handsome solo man a few feet away. He gives you a half-smile as he walks away.

Find a spot where you have auditory privacy, away from other people. Do not make the mistake of loudly sharing your intimate thoughts and problems with the world. Your loud laughs and exclamations, and the mere sound of frantic clicking, can invade another's space. (I discuss rules 1 and 3 at greater length below.)

Rule 4. The Tech Countdown

Do a body check and tech check. Notice how you're carrying, placing, and/or using your devices to make sure they don't make a dork statement, indicate your priorities incorrectly, or create a barrier between you and the people you're talking to.

Don't Be "Clued Out"

A strange nonverbal phenomenon occurs when we are connected via phone or electronic device. We feel such an intimate connection to the person we are directly communicating with that we give out nonverbal cues that we would normally reserve for one-on-one, intimate-space conversations. In addition, we tune out true environmental censors for our behavior. We no longer see, hear, or acknowledge the people in our *physical* space, so we don't follow the rules of etiquette for public communication.

Conversation puts a high cognitive load on the brain. When we focus on one sense, such as hearing, we lose much of our ability to monitor our environment with that sense and our other senses. Instead of being clued in we are clued out.

The technology itself and the public environments we now use it in can add to the problem. If we are on a smartphone, the poor sound quality can cause us to raise our voice on the call. In addition, my research on paralanguage, prosodics, and vocalics as they are transmitted through technology indicates that our inability to hear breathing and other vocal turn-taking signals when we are talking on phones in public places can make both caller and callee struggle for understanding, increase frustration, and make the users raise their voices. Recently, while I was sitting in the airport working on this book, a man sat down in the row of chairs across from me and in a loud voice began talking about how much his dead uncle loved drinking gin. As part of the auditory assault on all those around him, he hooted with laughter and methodically kicked the seat across from him, which was connected to my seat, jolting me every few minutes. I tried to get his attention to ask him to stop (or at least ask him what brand of gin his uncle preferred), but he was so engrossed in his conversation he was oblivious to his rudeness.

You may be wondering, "What does it matter? That man will never see you again. What difference does it make what kind of impression he makes?" In many instances, it won't make a difference to the perpetrator of inconsiderate behavior. But we've all seen movies and TV shows in which one person is rude to another person, only to find out that that person is her new boss or some other person who can make a significant impact on her life. That scenario isn't just fiction. You never know who the person witnessing your inconsiderate behavior may be.

A friend was standing in the lobby of a building and talking loudly on her cell phone. She continued her call in the crowded elevator, oblivious to everyone riding with her, until she went to step off on her floor and noticed several people glaring at her. She didn't think much about it, but later that day, when she met with her department heads and was introduced to a new manager, she saw that he was one of the people who'd been glaring at her in the elevator!

Not only is there the possibility of making a poor impression on someone who might be able to harm or benefit you in some way, but there's also a larger reason to be considerate in public: being considerate of others makes the world a better place for everyone. Less rudeness means less stress, and that means more peace. Who doesn't want *more* peace in the world?

Turn off your devices when you go to a meeting or other public event. You may doubt it's possible for you to so do. Anyone can live for a couple of hours without texting another person and without checking her email. (Leave the baby/device with a sitter if necessary.) You are not the president of the United States. No one is going to start a nuclear war — not one that you can prevent, anyway. So let it go and be in the moment.

A CEO who attended her company's presentation at a large national convention found that there were hundreds of decision makers, representing her company's prospective customers, in the banquet hall. Everyone at her company knew the stakes were high. If the presentation went well, those prospects might purchase her company's technology, earning the company millions of dollars in the next quarter. Imagine her dismay when she noticed key employees from her company texting on their smartphones during the presentation! She knew not only that they were making a poor first impression on the prospects but also that their behavior was contagious — prospects seated around the texters were texting as well. Needless to say, she snapped at her employees for their poor snaps, reprimanding all the texters publicly (by name) at their company meeting that night.

Everyone, it seems, has a horror story about behavior related to technology, from cell phones going off in the middle of a funeral to employees checking their Facebook pages in the middle of a meeting. Participants at my public speaking workshops want to know how to deal with people in meetings who are distracted by their electronic devices. Remember, it's not merely about you or their respect for you; its about them failing to show respect for every person in the room. When someone is talking, texting, or using his iPad while you're talking at a meeting or giving a speech, here's how to respond:

- First, try ignoring the person to see if the audience or team members will take care of it.
- Since the distracted person is often too distracted to notice he is being rude, you can silently signal displeasure with eye contact and by tapping him on the shoulder. Or you can make a hand gesture to someone seated next to the distracted person, signaling that she should get the offending person to stop. If you do this and you're standing, quickly move to another part of the room to continue your talk. If seated, look away from the offender, so the interaction doesn't embarrass the chastised tech abuser.
- Or, if you are standing, you can move next to the troublemaker. Don't make eye contact or chastise him; just continue speaking.

Email and Other Electronic Interactions

Many people are surprised to learn that emails and texts can communicate nonverbally. As technology increases, we need to be continually aware that each time we tap a key or swipe a finger across a screen, we are communicating. Following are the most important dos and don'ts.

Email is a nonverbal communication that gives others an impression of you. Your first email to someone should be as formal as if you were writing a letter. This is critical if you are sending business emails. Writing the salutation "Dear [name]" and then skipping a line before you start your message may seem old-fashioned, but there is a reason to do it. It lengthens the time it takes to get to the impersonal part of the message and formalizes the reader's initial first impression, so it makes you look more professional, more intelligent, and kinder. When your message is complete, writing a close like "Sincerely, [your name]" will also convey politeness, which is a wonderful recency effect. The recency effect, also called the "peak end rule," is the effect of the last thing you say or do. And it is a consequence of our tendency to give greater weight to recent events — what just happened, or what happened last — than to earlier events.

Keep your texts, email, and Facebook entries as direct and simple as you can. People in business may get hundreds of emails every day. Try not to make too many points. Bullet points are better than long paragraphs. If you need a response to particular questions, number your questions and ask the reader to add her reply directly following your question. If you write a paragraph, make it no more than two sentences. Write a short subject line that indicates what your email is about. If you've been clear in your subject line, you can save someone hours of time later when she's looking through all her emails trying to find that vital piece of information. And you want her to remember you fondly — not be cursing your name at midnight. Right now, check out your electronic devices and see how your subject lines read on the screens and how many characters they allow.

Proofread! Make sure your grammar and spelling are correct. Check to be certain you are sending the message to the correct person.

Be careful of the autocorrect function on your devices. Though there are hysterically funny website blogs and books dedicated to examples of autocorrect's propensity to change your ordinary misspelled words into embarrassing messages, you don't want your friends forwarding your texts for consideration for the next issue!

For a sample of how a first email to a client should look, see the sidebar below, "What a Good Email Snap Looks Like."

What a Good Email Snap Looks Like

Subject: Creating Your Graphics

Dear Ms. Jones:

I understand that you would like my company to produce graphics for your newsletter. We are happy to provide this service for you. Please feel free to call me or send me a description of what you are looking for, including:

- number of photos
- number of illustrations
- design specifications

When I have received this information, I will be able to send you a quote. I look forward to hearing from you

Sincerely,
Reginald Baker
President
All Graphics
cell: 404-555-1222

Once you have established contact with a person, you should still use a greeting of some sort, unless the email has turned into a back-and-forth conversation. Even then, I recommend that you use the person's name in the message. It creates a more personal interaction, and research shows that the use of names in texts and emails typically creates more follow-through on requests and less misunderstanding and conflict. For example, a follow-up email might look like this:

Re: Creating Your Graphics
Thanks, Reggie, for the information. I'll look into this right away.

Remember, you continue to create, or re-create, an impression with every email you send. So consider the following:

Be sure to read your email carefully before replying. You might want to number the topics you are responding to and create a numbered, boldface single word for each one so you know you have responded to each request.

Your response speed — or lack of response — gives an impression. Be sure to answer all professional and business emails in a timely manner. If you are unable to access your email for a particular period, you can create an autoresponse that explains how long you will be unavailable. Time is a powerful communicator. Some people's standard response is hours, while for others it's minutes or even seconds. Delays in responses affect the impression you give.

While we are on the subject of time, be aware that the hour at which you send an email is time-stamped next to your message. Sometimes it's great to impress someone with your workaholic tendencies by replying to their requests at 2 AM, and sometimes it makes it look as if you don't get enough sleep.

When You Don't Want to Email Back and Forth Ad Nauseam

Have you wondered when to end a text conversation? Perhaps you've been afraid that if you didn't respond you'd be perceived negatively? Make it easy for people to know that you don't require a response, by using an abbreviation I created for my clients to employ within their companies: *AG*. This stands for "It's all good; there is no need to respond." Add *AG* to both the subject line and the end of your email.

Once others understand the concept, you can also use the abbreviation *GOT*, which stands for "I got your message, I read it, I understand it, and I approve of it," or *GOTDO*, which stands for that plus "I will follow through."

Most professionals use a signature block, or "sig line," to close their emails. The signature should include your name, title, company name, and contact information. Be careful of being cutesy with your sig line; and check the spelling before you create one. I had been using a new signature line for two months before a potential client mentioned that the word *professional* was misspelled in it. Not very professional!

Be careful of what you delete as well as what you send. When I did consulting for an Internet security company, I discovered that there is software that can be run on your emails and documents to recover everything you entered, including all your deleted text, and all the original documents you accessed to create it.

When you receive a group email, you usually need not reply to all. Make sure you are not cluttering up other people's email boxes when you could easily just reply to the sender (if even that is necessary). You'll create a bad impression on other members of the group when they see that your email has no relevance to them.

Check online often to see what first impression you're giving others. Search your name, search your name/photo, and search your name/video. Don't be surprised that your Aunt Caroline has a photo of you as a teenager in braces in front of the Christmas tree. You can request that your photo or video be taken off any website.

Think Ahead

In the freshman orientation at Emory University in Atlanta, the students are shown Facebook photo postings of kids their age in various embarrassing situations. One girl is shown bleary-eyed in yellow duck-covered pajamas in front of her dorm, another has his arms around two girls and is holding a vodka bottle, and a third is standing on a table dancing in her college sweatshirt and not much else. Students need to be aware that their expensive education could be wasted if photos on Facebook show up in a search by their prospective employers.

(Go to www.snapfirstimpressions.com for tools and information to help fix the impression you give people online.)

Social Media

We use things like Facebook as personal tools, but we also use them for networking. Facebook is a great place to share your favorite videos or quotes. It's a bad place to complain or to air your dirty laundry. Keep your status updates fairly impersonal and upbeat. By impersonal I don't mean you can't share good news — weddings, trips, or a good movie you've seen.

Media consultant Eileen Spiegler suggests people do some reading on how various social networks operate before posting any personal info. For instance, Facebook allows you to set much more restrictive limits on who has access to your postings. On Twitter, in contrast, essentially your only privacy option is to block followers — not the best way to ingratiate yourself with the community network you are presumably trying to participate in. Consider that anything you "tweet" will be visible to many people you don't know, and once it's in the webosphere, it's there *forever*. "Before becoming active in a social network," Spiegler says, "it's a good idea to do an online search of yourself to see what info is already out there." This "can be very sobering." Be aware that "sites like Spokeo.com list addresses, phone numbers, and other personal details, available

Twitter Rehab?

Writer Larry Carlat has written about his Twitter obsession, which grew from "trying to make a few friends laugh" to "posting 20 to 30 times a day, seven days a week." He did this for three years and "while driving, between sets of tennis, even at the movies" — until he realized his "entire life revolved around tweeting."

Eight months after he'd begun tweeting, Carlat started a new job. Though he'd removed his name from his Twitter feed before starting the job, someone in HR stumbled on his tweets and found they violated the company's social media policy.

Eventually, after an intervention of sorts by his young son, and after Carlat decided that his Twitter habit had "started to feel less like a rush and more like a burden," Carlat shut down his Twitter account, committing "Twittercide."[6]

in a simple search. Stay cognizant by doing occasional online searches of your name," Spiegler says.

Twitter's popularity may not last forever, but virtual interaction before and during events is the new normal. Before my presentations, for example, my clients often start a virtual conversation with people who will be attending the meeting. If you join a Twitter session, you have the chance to gather and send casual snaps.

I recently spoke on deception detection to the forensic science classes at a local private school. My audience was an incredible group of kids — warm, engaged, and brimming with curiosity and great questions. The atmosphere of the school is very much like that of a big family. The kids laugh and hug each other in the halls. I told the science teacher I wanted to live there!

I noticed that all students had to drop their cell phones and such into a box as they came into the classroom (a practice I

Technics of Rabbits or Turtles

Rabbits send lots of short emails, quick bursts of text that they expect immediate, brief responses to.

Turtles love emails and texts, but they are slower to respond and may agonize over the wording, spending much longer crafting each message and waiting to send it.

also see at college campuses and client meetings). I wanted to know how technology was affecting their lives. The best news is they still want to know how to tell if a girl or guy likes them; the fun news is they want to know how to tell this not just from their body language but also from their texts and other technic.

Rabbit or Turtle; or, He Loves Me, He Loves Me Not

One of the concepts I mentioned earlier is the pacing of messages. As I noted in the section "Matching Breath and Pacing" in chapter 5, rabbits and turtles have different pacing styles. A person's pacing can give you insights into her personality. After you discover her baseline pacing style, you can get further check-in impressions from the pacing of her email, texting, and Facebook exchanges, which will reflect changing dynamics in your relationship with her. So if a friend or colleague who usually responds in moments takes a long time to get back in touch, or changes from slow responses to quick responses, this is a form of nonverbal information.

There is also a larger effect of adjustable conversing speed. Email, texting, and Facebook communication is *asynchronous*, meaning the rate at which you converse is maneuverable. A conversation may occur over the course of minutes, days, weeks, or months. Interactive time can be shortened or stretched, as needed. And with Facebooking, there is a permanent record of the ebb and flow.

The Black Hole

You and someone else are sending messages back and forth, when suddenly there is a drastic drop in messages or they stop altogether. You stare at the screen trying to guess the reasons for the change. You reread messages looking for clues. Does the silence mean anger, indifference, withdrawal, or passive-aggressive punishment? Inside the agony of this ambiguity — the black hole — we project our own expectations, emotions, and anxieties, and, oddly, we don't often choose the obvious action, which is to talk to the person!

When someone does not respond to our techno messages, it may seem reasonable to assume they are busy. But we don't. We have had something and now we have nothing, so we fill in the resulting black hole with things like an imagined massive power outage, dire flood, or small volcanic eruption that prevents the other person from responding to us. Imagining molten lava keeping someone you care about from writing to you beats thinking you aren't the be-all and end-all.

The problem is, be it a work or personal relationship, without the other person there in front of you, you don't know for sure if he is wading through floodwaters to get his iPhone charged so he can call you or sipping a coffee at Starbucks with someone else, with his electronic device fully charged, within reach, and purposefully turned off.

Don't assume the worst. When in doubt, don't anguish, and for goodness sake don't send a worried or angry text or email. Remember, face-to-face communication gives you more emotional nuances, and a phone call is the fallback.

General Tech Etiquette

Focus on the other person before you focus on yourself. Whether in a phone call, an email, or a text, ask about the person you're addressing, or make a statement about him before you talk about yourself or make a request. This creates rapport. When you are pressed for time and overworked, it is so easy to start the conversation with "I need..." Remember, you invaded his visual or auditory space to communicate, so acknowledge him first. Start today. Try asking something simple like "How is your day?" or "What is the view out your window today?"

Think about what the other person would expect. Susan had graduated from college a year earlier and was still jobless and living with her parents. She had what she felt was a great phone interview from a PR firm in search of a client representative, which she considered her dream job. After the interview, she sent a brief professional email thanking the interviewer. Two weeks later, she still hadn't heard from the firm. She was upset and puzzled. I asked her to think about what skill set the person they wanted to hire would have. Would their PR client rep send a single email to a media source and wait two weeks to get a callback? Wouldn't this person call, I asked, and perhaps send hard-mail messages? Wouldn't this rep do everything possible to communicate in order to get the job done?

If there is a conflict or misunderstanding, or you need something important now, use more than one form of communication to ensure understanding and create a good relationship. Send emails and voice mails, stop by her office, and make sure she got the information. Different people process information differently. Some people are visual and will read email, some are auditory and will listen on the phone, some are kinesthetic and want human contact and physical anchors. Even if the business culture or a set of friends engages in texting all the time, this doesn't mean the person you're dealing with does. Keep in mind that different cultures (such as work, family, or friends) require different types of language and sometimes different communication devices. Follow the lead of others, and always do your best to keep your messages short and on point, since many people won't bother to read a long email or listen to a rambling voice mail.

Telephone Tips

Have a professional message on your work, home, and cell phone voice mail. Speak clearly and don't speak too fast. Give a sufficient amount of information and no more. Avoid music, slang, and funny voices.

Leave professional messages on voice mail. Realize that fewer and fewer people listen to their voice mail messages, so if you leave a voice mail, follow up with email

Count to Ten

Sara, a consultant with a nationally recognized accounting firm, was driving from Philadelphia to New York after a hard week of work on the road. In five o'clock traffic her cell phone rang — it was an important call from a client Sara had just met for the first time. The new client began a heated complaint about one of Sara's coworkers. Sara, already stressed, "freaked out." Fearing that her company would lose the client, she started listing her own complaints, matching the voice tone and tempo of her client. That night as she was going to sleep, she realized her mistake: she had left her coworker high and dry. Even though she apologized to both her coworker and the client, she still feels bad. "I learned a valuable lesson," she told me. "There are times when you should not take a call, even if it seems important."

or a text. Prepare your message before you call. Make it short but complete. Leave your full name, your phone number, and your email address. Always say why you called. If you have more than one point to make, say at the very beginning of the call, "I am calling about two issues."

Cell phones can catch you casual and harried. Be careful when answering your cell phone on the fly. If your business colleagues call you on your cell, don't answer when you can't speak clearly and calmly. Be aware that if you are in the car, your mind is distracted, and some states prohibit or regulate cell phone use while driving. Also realize that if you answer the phone while in the bathroom, the echo bouncing off the tile is distinctly noticeable.

Be fully present and connected. When you're on the phone, you lose much of the expressiveness you would normally communicate face-to-face with nonverbal cues, so you have to ramp up the energy level to get your enthusiasm across. If you can, stand up and use your natural body movement and gestures to keep your delivery real and your energy high.

Multitasking

My friend Steve has attention deficit disorder. People with ADD have a hard time staying focused, but they pride themselves on their ability to shift from one thing to another easily. One day Steve was driving with a friend, engaged in a great conversation, when he realized he'd missed his exit. He apologized to his friend, saying that he must have been distracted by their conversation.

"I thought you said ADD'ers can do several things at one time," said Steve's companion.

"I did," said Steve. "But I didn't say we do them well."

Just because you can do several things at one time — drive, pay attention to the road, talk on the phone, listen to the traffic report — doesn't mean you can do those things well. With all our technology, we think we're accomplishing more in less time, when in reality we are setting ourselves up for mistakes and poor communication. What makes it worse is that, while other people notice, you're so busy multitasking that you don't.

A CEO of a large company based in Miami, Florida, told me, "It's getting out of hand. I wish I could have lockers for all my employees and make them lock up their cell phones before they come in to work. I feel like a school principal rather than a business owner, asking my employees to work instead of talking on the phone, texting, and going online!"

What do your boss and coworkers think of your gadgets? Once again, just because "everyone is doing it," this doesn't make it the thing to do. You'll stand out in a positive way if you don't.

Techno Impressions and Trust

A 2008 study that appeared in *Organizational Behavior and Human Decision Processes* showed that the speed of firing off emails and engaging in video conferences may result in doing things fast but the results may cost you more than time. Gregory Northcraft of the University of Illinois says high-tech communication undermines the personal interaction needed to breed trust, which is vital in teamwork: "Technology has made us much more efficient, but much less effective."[7]

Under Northcraft's direction, more than two hundred undergraduate students took part in two hypothetical teamwork exercises, some face-to-face and others through email and video conferences. Face-to-face contact yielded the most trust and cooperation, while email netted the least, with video conferences somewhere in between. Talking about his research, Northcraft said, "Face to face, people just have more confidence that others will do what they say they'll do. Over e-mail, they trust each other less."

One of my clients, the head of an international sales team with the top sales in the company, shared one of his secrets to making a good impression. "I mix it up. I call my salespeople and clients; I meet with my salespeople and ride along with them on their sales calls. I email and I text. I also send personal handwritten notes. I don't just do the easy thing or get in a rut. I want to connect on a human level, not share data."

Next time somebody's phone rings during an important meeting or during a speech or important conversation, notice the expressions on other people's faces. The expressions say everything you need to know about the snap impressions people get when we use technology to a fault. If the only thing you know about a person is that he is glued to his electronic devices, your snap of him is likely to be negative.

Technology allows us to connect more quickly and sometimes more efficiently with others. But it will never replace the impression we leave through a personal, face-to-face conversation. Be smart about and aware of the way you're using technology for communication. It can affect your relationships in a snap.

7. HOW YOU LOOK TO OTHERS IN A SNAP

See What Others See in You and Get a First-Impression Makeover

The first time I met Brian, he greeted me with a warm hand shake, a smile, and spinach between his teeth. I reacted like any decent person would. I smiled back, exposing my teeth like a gopher and pantomimed brushing my teeth with my finger. Brian got the hint and then continued our meeting spinachless. Years later, Brian still tells that story. "What if you hadn't done that?" he asked me. "What if you'd thought, 'What a loser,' and rebuffed me? What if I had gotten home, looked in the mirror, and realized I had spinach between my teeth?"

We are often unaware of the first impression we make. People form them in a snap, but they don't usually tell you about them. We can walk around clueless about how we really look to others. We wonder why we can't sell to a client or get a date with a hottie, or why we feel awkward in a meeting or at a party. The truth is, everyone walks around with big blind spots when it comes to their nonverbal behaviors. And as awkward as it is to realize you met someone when you had spinach between your teeth, dog hair on your jacket, or a price tag hanging off the back your pants, it is also difficult and awkward not knowing you have nonverbal behaviors that make people respond to you in certain negative ways. Even if people aren't staring at your teeth, handing you a lint brush, or pulling a price tag from your pants, you can gain insight into, and feedback about, how you look to others — and figure out what you need to change.

We've looked at dozens of body language cues that people process in a snap as they form first impressions. Let's now look more closely at the question we all have: How do I look to others? And as you take a thorough look at the impressions you make on others, you'll learn how you can improve those first impressions, and even how to get a second chance to make a first impression.

In this chapter, you will learn the importance of knowing how you appear from other people's perspective. You will

- examine how you *think* you look — your self-perception;
- understand what your viewable first-impression behaviors are;
- uncover the true first impression that you make; and
- practice making your best first impression on others.

I thought I gave others a great first impression. Fresh out of graduate school and very young and naive, I went to work for a consulting company in a big downtown office building. After working in academia, I'd already owned a successful speaking and training business. I brought my clients with me to the consulting company and continued to generate my own business.

It was a small firm, with fewer than forty consultants and staff members. The consultants had no official office hours or meetings they had to attend. You came in when you wanted to, did what you wanted to do, and left whenever. I was on the road almost every week giving speeches and conducting training programs, and usually flew back late at night, so I rarely got to the office before 10 AM. I would say hello to the person at the front desk, visit with the support staff near the door, and then go immediately to my little back-corner office, close the door, and start working.

Petite and blonde, I looked like a twelve-year-old if I wasn't dressed to the nines. So when I spoke to audiences, I always dressed professionally, wore high heels, and devoted an hour to my hair, makeup, and nails. (Yes, an hour; insane but true.) After a week on the road spent speaking, I didn't want to dress for the office. So I went casual. The other consultants wore suits, while the staff dressed casually, since clients didn't come into the office. I worked until 4 PM and then took a lunch break. I did not "visit" my coworkers or stand in the hallway talking about my new clients or new techniques, and I didn't accept offers to lunch with my coworkers. I was too busy working.

The entire downtown building cleared out at 5 PM on the dot. I usually stayed in the otherwise empty office until 8 or 9 PM and then Mac, the security guy, kindly escorted me from the building to my car. The company was going through some hard times, so I took more jobs than I personally needed to take and traveled a heck of a lot more than any sane person should. I worked so much that I had no life other than work. As far as I knew, I was the only person bringing cash flow to the company.

So I was puzzled when none of my coworkers ever brought me in on their long-term projects. In my *self-perception*, I was making a great impression. I was working like a dog for the team and was bringing in business; I got rave reviews from my clients. So why wasn't I getting projects internally?

One day, I was in the office making sales calls, which was always fun. I knew my clients well, and I would spend sales days laughing and visiting on the phone. Oddly, a new consultant to the firm who specialized in sales kept going back and forth in front of my office. I could hear him; I even opened the door and asked him if he needed me. But he smiled and shook his head no. As it neared 4 PM, I gathered up the notes from all the business I had booked and carried them down to my assistant so she could send the contracts. Then I went to the break room, where the new sales consultant found me — casually dressed, sitting on the chair with my legs and feet folded up under me, reading a magazine and munching on a fajita salad.

"Hey. All day I could hear you laughing through my office wall, making all those personal calls. You were having so much fun," he said.

I thought I had heard wrong and said, "Excuse me?"

"I'm not going to tell anyone you were making personal calls all day. I just wanted to rib you."

I was shocked and managed to stammer out, "No, I was making sales calls today."

"Sure you were," he joked. "So was I."

"No, I was really making sales calls. I just took notes for four contracts down to get their packets sent out today!"

Now it was his turn to be surprised. He paused for quite a while and then said, "That's how you make sales calls?" Suddenly,

---

The Value of Check-Ins

Remember: You create a check-in first impression at the beginning of every workday, at the beginning of every meeting, and at the beginning of every phone call or other interaction. People check in to see how you are going to be on that particular day and in that particular situation. And on the basis of the check-in, they decide how they will treat you. Think of the times you looked at someone and thought, "Wow, he is in a bad mood. I'd better be careful."

If you want to change your overall snap, then focus on each of your check-ins to establish new behaviors. The good news is that the more interactions you have, and the more check-ins you do in different environments (in and out of the office, for example), the greater your chance of improving your overall snap. A simple way to find out if you're making the changes you want to make is to do a check-in on your own behavior at the beginnings and endings of interactions.

my professional career flashed before my eyes. To this sales trainer and to everyone in the office, I was the little blonde who came in late, looking casual, and laughed on the phone all day. No wonder they did not see me as a professional. By the nonverbal behaviors they could see, I wasn't.

It turned out that nobody but the office manager knew I was bringing in money; my hard work, late nights, and excellent critiques from clients were *invisible* behaviors. The company had stopped sharing profit information and client feedback in Friday morning meetings — meetings I missed because I came in later. I had messed up royally! I was teaching nonverbal communication, but forgot I was communicating every time I went into the office, and communicating even when I didn't show up. I thought, "I already know these guys. I have made my first impression, and from now on, my work should speak for my professionalism." I didn't recognize that you create a check-in first impression at the beginning of every workday, at the beginning of every meeting, and at the beginning of every phone call or other interaction.

EXERCISE

From Behavior to Impression

Imagine the check-in first impression I gave to my coworkers each day. Do that by considering the *viewable behaviors* my coworkers saw. Each day they saw someone who was late to work, dressed casually, stayed behind a closed door, didn't share ideas or client leads, laughed on the phone all day, didn't go to meetings, and sat with her feet folded under her. What impression would you have formed?

EXERCISE

From Impression to Behavior

Think of someone you are not fond of. This can be a person you know — an acquaintance, a coworker, a family member — or someone in the media spotlight, like a celebrity, politician, or news personality. Now think of your first impression of that person, and list three to five nonverbal behaviors. Make sure that you list specific behaviors — things they do and/or the way they do them — not your perceptions. Did these *behaviors* lead to your negative impression of the person?

Changing the Impression You Make

There is a classic makeover TV show called *What Not to Wear*. Each episode focuses on one person whose friends and family members, appalled at how he or she dresses, have proposed that he or she be given a makeover. I find the show entertaining on many levels. Why are the bad dressers always so surprised they were chosen for the show? Apparently their friends and family never told them. Or they didn't believe what they were told. Or they didn't know what it takes to make a good first impression.

Do you have anything in common with the women and men on the show? Think about it. Most of your friends and family are strangely uncomfortable telling you what's wrong with you. (Except perhaps your mother and your spouse, but that's a different book.) Yet they all formed opinions of your wardrobe, hair, and so on the first time, or one of the first few times, they saw them. Let's say they make a face when you wear that too-tight shirt, but they don't say, "You cannot wear that anymore. You have gotten too fat!" Or, if people do tell you, you ignore it. You think, "But it's my favorite shirt." Or you think, "I have always looked good in this shirt. In fact, ever since junior high, I have looked hot in this!" You may not know what snappy dressing or a good first impression looks like.

On the show, the fashion consultants put the guests in a four-way mirror booth so they can see themselves from all sides. That alone is painful for the guest. Then the consultants come in and start coaching. They are *brutally* honest, saying things like, "You look horrible in that," "That color is awful with your hair color," and "These shoes went out when you were in high school, or they were never in." Then they give tips on good dressing and even use mannequins dressed appropriately to show some examples of outfits that would look good on the person they're coaching. Finally, they have the person go out and use the tips to shop for clothes.

You may not be a terrible dresser or have horrible body language, but there may be things you don't know about yourself. If you want to improve your body language, you need to get in the middle of a metaphorical four-way mirror that will show you your behavior, and then be brutally honest with yourself, find models of the best nonverbal behaviors, and change the behaviors that affect the snap impression you give others.

What follows is an exercise that will help you see what *others* see when they first look at you. I created the exercise for myself the day the sales guy talked to me in the break room. I needed something — a four-way-mirrored booth — to help me see the gap between how I saw myself and how others saw me. I made three lists, detailing how I viewed myself, my viewable behaviors, and what anyone viewing such behaviors would think of the person who engaged in them.

This exercise changed my life. Workshop participants and my corporate and coaching clients have told me over the years that it has changed their lives, too, by helping them see their blind spots and learn how others view them. Reread my story

Invisible Behaviors: Making Your Work Known

There are so many things you do that could show your effort, your credibility, and your likability, but that other people don't see. You may be spending hours on work that others know nothing about. In a business setting, changing others' perceptions of you may require not only that you spend more viewable time with other people but also that you tell them what you are working on. You may think this is bragging, but in reality it is communicating. Making the unknown known to others increases the opportunity for them to like you, admire you, and — in the business world — see the potential for giving you both raises and more responsibility. So visit other people's offices, and go out to lunch with leaders.

about myself as a new employee. As you do this, think of the impression you give others, and then do the "Snap Me" exercise that follows.

Context matters. Think of how you really are in each situation. I thought I was professional because I behaved that way when I was with my clients, but the impression I gave in the office was different. We may think we are warm and caring because we are that way with our families, but we may not really give that impression to our customers. We might think we are hard-driving professionals because we get through 342 emails and 200 texts a day, but when the boss walks into our cubicles, we may present ourselves as bleary eyed and half asleep.

EXERCISE

Snap Me

Take out a sheet of paper (or go to www.snapfirst impressions.com for the online worksheet; you will also find sample lists that let you compare your answers to those of others). Create three columns. Label the first column "Self-Perceptions," the second "Viewable Behaviors," and the last one "Others' Perceptions."

1. In the first column, write a list of your *self-perceptions* — all the things you believe to be true of you. What is your personality? What are your characteristics?

    If you work for an employer, list all the things you believe to be true about yourself as an employee, supervisor, or coworker. My list in the story would have said, "Professional, workaholic, great speaker, team player," and so on.

    Then, in the same column, make a list of how you see yourself in personal situations — say, as a spouse, parent, and friend. The list should include personality characteristics, adjectives and adverbs that describe what you believe about yourself. Examples might include *happy*, *strong*, *overbearing*, *calm*, *friendly*, and *shy*.

2. In the second column, write down your *viewable behaviors* — all the things that others see you say and do. Typically, the items in this column are the things you do with friends, coworkers, dates, customers, or clients while face-to-face, while on the phone, or through email and texts — things they are likely to have noticed. You must be honest with yourself here. To give you an idea, my list included my way-too-casual clothes, my bad hair, not saying hello to my coworkers, my messy desk, and my childlike habit of sitting on my feet at meetings (the few I did go to). List only the behaviors others see and hear, not what you think they mean. For example, when listing your work behaviors, write everything that your team sees you do. Don't write down anything you do behind closed doors or that you tell others you do — only the things they actually see you doing. I couldn't write down that I got standing ovations from audiences and great

critiques from clients. Those things were invisible and, frankly, irrelevant to my office coworkers.

List all these items as nonverbal behaviors, and be specific. These should be things a scientist looking at your life would write down in her lab notes. For example, instead of writing down "friendly," as you did on your self-perception list, write viewable behaviors, such as "They see me come into work every day and say hello to everyone with a smile on my face and cheery voice." Instead of "business-like," write, "They see me grumpy and sour faced, hunched over my computer, until I have my coffee" or "They see me go directly to my computer and start working without stopping to smile or wave at anyone." Instead of "workaholic" you might write, "They see the long rambling emails I send at two in the morning or they typically see me with a cup of coffee in my hand rushing somewhere or with my head down texting."

For a work situation, think about the following:

- How and when do you come into work each day? (Remember, time is a powerful nonverbal communicator.) What do you do nonverbally? And what, if anything do you say to people? Include what you say in the parking lot, the elevator, the hallway. What is your first behavior that your coworkers see? If you are working on the first impression you give to clients, customers, prospective dates, friends, or family members, think of that first visual interaction in a specific context and list your behaviors.

- How do you usually dress, from your shoes up to your head? Be sure you use descriptive words for your clothes, shoes, jewelry, glasses, watches, wallets, phones, bags, and accessories, such as *pressed, wrinkled, old, tight, big, in style, dated, scuffed, crisply pressed, worn,* and so on.

- What does your office or cubicle, and especially your desk, look like?
- What are your standard everyday nonverbal facial expressions and voice like?
- How often do you work in your cubicle or any other place where others can see you?
- Do you keep your back to the entrance of your office or cubicle?
- How do you sit — what is your typical posture like when you are working and not working?
- How do you respond when others come into your office, cubicle, or other work area?
- Do you visit others, and if you do, what is your nonverbal behavior then?
- How do you respond to phone calls, emails, and texts: quickly, slowly, never, abruptly?
- How do you answer your phone, and how do you talk on it?
- What are your lunch behavior and break room behavior like? Where do you sit, and how do you eat? Who do you talk to, and who don't you talk to?
- What is your behavior at meetings — when do you arrive, and where do you sit?
- What is your one-on-one and big-meeting behavior? Do you listen, speak, or doodle?
- How quickly or slowly do you respond to requests? (Response time is a nonverbal communicator.)
- How do you treat different people — coworkers, your boss, clients, and customers?

- How and when do you leave work each day? Do you say good-bye?
- Do you socialize after work? If so, what do you do?

3. In the third and last column, list other people's perceptions of you. First, look closely at all those viewable behaviors from their point of view. What would you say about another person you saw doing those things, especially if those were the only behaviors you ever saw? Now take some time and write down these snap impressions. Be judgmental. For me, this step was a revelation. No wonder I wasn't pulled in on projects! The other guys didn't even know who I was or what I could do. I was just a laughing, casually dressed kid. What is your objective perception of your own behaviors? If you like, you can show the second column to other people and ask them what they would think of that person. Take it to your boss and see what he says. Sit down with your sweetie and best friend and see what they say.

4. Now compare the first column, "Self-Perceptions," with the third column, "Others' Perceptions." How do your perceptions of yourself compare with their perceptions of you? Are you coming across the way you think you do? Are you coming across the way you want to?

5. Finally, make a list of actions you are willing to change if you need to, and behaviors you should continue if they are creating the impression you want. Changing impressions may include letting your positive invisible behaviors — such as the great speech you gave outside the office, or your

sense of humor that only comes out when you're relaxed — be known to others. It may also include creating opportunities to spend time with people in a variety of situations.

Set up courageous conversations. If you are working on altering others' perceptions of you at work, set up a meeting with coworkers, your team leader, your boss, or your clients. Ask them, "What is or was your first impression of me?" "What specific behaviors led you to that impression?" *Getting truthful feedback is difficult.* If they give positive feedback, ask, "How can I give others an even better impression?" If they say, "It was fine," or give you other nebulous or nonspecific feedback, ask, "What would be one specific thing I can change to make a great impression?" or "What am I doing now that I could do even better?" Whatever you hear, listen quietly and say thank you. Don't try to defend yourself or explain your actions. They have given you a gift. Believe me, there are people in your life who are just dying to tell you that you have spinach between your teeth. You just need to ask.

Tooting Your Own Horn

Carol shared the following with me: "I spent years being mad that I was passed over for projects and promotions. Then I realized that my managers didn't know what part of the team's projects were my work, or how great I was with top clients when I was on the road with them. I started going out to lunch with my managers, and when they mentioned things that they were doing well, I could toot my own horn a bit. Who knew there was all this horn blowing going on?"

How It Works

A client gave me this bit of feedback: "I was intrigued by your story that you call all your clients at the beginning of the new year and ask about your first impression, seeking honest feedback. After the 'Snap Me' exercise, you gave everyone on the sales team homework, asking them to have courageous conversations with our prospects and clients.

"I really didn't believe you could get people to tell you the truth. But I started making the calls and asking for feedback, and it was amazing. I found out I was rushing my calls and giving the impression I was impatient, and that some people even thought I was angry when I answered the phone. I've slowed down and don't bark out my hello, and this has already made a difference."

EXERCISE

Modeling Your Best Person

Here is another exercise that can help you improve the first impression you give others. Imagine yourself as the best person you can possibly be. It's important to have real-life models of the characteristics you want. Then you can look at those people and see the behaviors to model.

Make a list of all the people you admire. They can be people you have known personally, famous leaders, celebrities, or fictional characters in movies and books. Three of the people on my list are Oprah Winfrey, Ted Clevenger (former dean of communication at Florida State University), and my friend Sarah. If you have trouble making a list, let it simmer on the back burner for a while. As you go to sleep each night during the following week, ask yourself to dream about people you admire and wish to emulate. (For lists of people who give a great snap impression, and for blogs about great snappers, go to www.snapfirst impressions.com.) Once you have your list, write down those admirable people's characteristics too. This is what my list looked like:

- Oprah — honesty, sincerity, and sense of humor
- Ted Clevenger — honesty, sincerity, integrity, intelligence, the ability to read people, warmth, and compassion
- My friend Sarah — honesty, intelligence, sense of humor, and warmth

Now look at your list of people and characteristics and write down what each of these people does to *show* that he or she has these characteristics. Go deep. It is easy for us to think of how someone dresses. Do that, and then go on to their actions. I asked myself, "What does Oprah do on her network that conveys her sincerity?" What is it about each of the people on *your* list that you like and wish to emulate: the voice, posture, leaning, gestures, touch, use of time, how he or she greets others and enters and exits a room, eye contact, and mouth behaviors? As you make this list, see if any of the nonverbal behaviors of one person are shared by a different person on the list, and put a tick mark next to each one you find.

Now you have a list of ideal behaviors. And you know exactly where successfully doing those behaviors will lead. If you practice those behaviors, you will be one of the most admirable people you know.

(For examples and other exercises — such as one that will help you figure out how the five people you spend the most time with affect your snap — go to www.snapfirstimpressions.com.)

Lack of Face-to-Face Time

I'm sure you will agree with me that there is less face-to-face communication than there was even ten years ago. We talk to our friends and family members on our smartphones, read texts, play games on our computer screens, and stare at televisions, all with our hearts and heads and eyes turned toward a screen rather than toward each other. Whatever happened to looking into someone's eyes?

Speaking of looking into someone's eyes, people don't even need to meet in person anymore to begin the dating process. Of the ten million Internet users who said they were single and looking for partners in 2006, 74 percent used the Internet to further their romantic interests in one way or another, and 37 percent actually visited a dating website. According to a Pew study, these two groups of users combined represent 10 percent of *all* Internet users that year.[1] Both Match.com and eHarmony .com currently claim to have 20 million registered users.

Business colleagues complain they don't get to meet potential clients. The customer goes to their website, clicks on a button that says, "Send me information," and then asks for pricing by email. Nobody gets to take the full measure of the other person in this kind of business interaction.

The brain needs and *expects* the other — more significant — channels of information provided by facial and vocal feedback. As I mentioned earlier, the brain suffers when it doesn't get in-person readings, and so does the communication. The neuroscientist Dr. Thomas Lewis suggests that we need *immediate facial feedback* to feed the brain and allow us to empathize, so we can understand others. In our texting, tweeting, Facebooking world, he says, "no matter how much we practice communicating through text, the brain still finds it stressful."[2]

Various reports say that parents now spend an average of only one hour a week in face-to-face contact with their children! That means one hour a week to pick up on cues that would let us know how everyone in the family is doing. With so little time together, and when the time they do have is so rushed, how do parents even know when there's a problem with their children? And how do children get the immediate nonverbal feedback that makes them feel seen, heard, and understood — and helps them practice empathy?

There are countless nonverbal cues — a door shut loudly, a late arrival home, a love song that's hummed, a forward lean, a touch on the arm, a sigh, averted eyes, a meal partially eaten — that can help us understand and nurture our social relationships.

I was sitting at the dinner table with my friends Kevin and Amy and their daughters, six-year-old Shannon and two-year-old Rachel. Kevin raised his voice ever so slightly and said, "Shannon, it's not your turn to talk. Your mother was talking." Amy leaned over her two-year-old's high chair, touched the side of the girl's head lovingly and said sternly, "Rachel, don't talk with your mouth open. Finish chewing, and then talk."

Kevin and Amy then turned in their chairs and leaned

What Makes Someone Appear Selfish or Narcissistic

Selfishness occurs when someone assesses his own emotions as being always and everywhere more valid than the emotions of others — like a kid who wants the other kid's toy, and takes it. In its extreme, this is narcissism. "Hot" narcissists have trouble regulating their overwhelming emotions, such as anger, sadness, and happiness. For example, they may get mad or happy very quickly at seemingly insignificant incidents, or be unable to understand the pain of others. In some cases, they have a need to make their emotions bigger and more important than another's.

The emotions of "cold" narcissists are not that strong, but their ability to inhibit actions is insufficient. Since they do not feel emotions as strongly as most people do, they may go after other things, such as money, power, drugs, or sex, in order to "feel," but without seeing that the snap impressions they give may look cold or abusive to others. They are unable to see how their actions or attitude can affect the lives of others.

forward toward Shannon, giving her their full attention as Kevin said, "Tell us what you did in school today." Shannon's face broke into a smile as wide as a watermelon wedge, and she began talking about the art project she did. Her parents' interest did not waver as they nodded their heads and kept asking her questions. They didn't even take a bite of food until Shannon threw up her hands and said, "That's all!"

Kevin turned to me and asked where I had been traveling. I said "Florida." Little Shannon turned in her chair, made direct eye contact, and asked loudly, "Did you go swimming a lot?" I answered, "Yes," marveling that a six-year-old knew how to ask follow-up questions, and that she modeled my excitement by bobbing her head and mirroring my facial expressions as I described swimming and floating on a raft over the ocean waves.

As I sat there, I was impressed by the constant, gentle corrections and sweet encouragements. I had noticed this each month when I had dinner with them, but this night I started counting the instances of verbal and nonverbal coaching just as I would do in research and consulting projects. I stopped when I got to twenty-two coaching statements or nonverbal corrections, such as a raised eyebrow of reproach or a nod of approval.

You may know about the research that shows a strong relationship between teen dropout rates and drug use and how many times a family eats dinner together. It seems like such a small thing, but nonverbal communication is a language, a very complex language, and to learn it well as a child you need adult modeling and corrections and practice over and over again. In fact, research indicates that children can and do learn body language by having family dinner together at least three times a week for eighteen years. This allows them to produce and strengthen neural pathways to social centers of their brain and, consequently, improve their interpersonal skills.

I have been polling my audiences for many years and recording their responses to various questions. When I say, "Raise your
hand if you had dinner with your family growing up," I find that
in some audiences filled with people under twenty-five, no one
raises a hand. And then we wonder why people under twenty-
five may rather text us than talk to us! It takes eighteen years of
face-to-face interaction with adults to learn all the intricacies
of the nonverbal language. Below are some exercises I do with
my corporate clients that you can do too. These can show you a
direct relationship between your family conversation and dinner habits, on the one hand, and your behaviors in meetings
and group discussions in your adult life, on the other. In your
family, make use of this face time to communicate verbally and
nonverbally and to model and observe good interpersonal and
nonverbal communication.

EXERCISE

The Table Test, Past and Present

Draw a picture of the dinner table your family had
while you were growing up. Put your name by the
seat where you ate, and then write in the names of
everyone else. If you ate in front of the TV or your laptop, draw that. Now draw lines between who talked to
whom the most. Then imagine your body language,
your voice at the dinner table, and the body language
of others.

- What were your nonverbal behaviors at the table?
- What were other people's nonverbal behaviors?
- How did others treat you and interact with you?
- How did you feel at the family dinner table?

Now draw how and where you tend to sit at meeting, dinners, and conference tables as an adult and where other people sit in those settings.

- How do you act at meetings today?
- How do other people interact with you?

Are there any similarities between your behavior as a child and your adult behaviors and relationships when you are sitting around a conference table or are out to dinner?

- How do you feel about your snap in each of those settings?
- What would you like to improve about your snap?

You may want to go back to chapter 2 and look at the four first-impression factors and see how they affect your snap.

(Go to www.snapfirstimpressions.com for the Table Test online worksheet and examples.)

High Anxiety

One little-discussed by-product of a lack of body language skills is nervousness, fear, a lack of confidence, and the kind of anxiety so many of us now treat with medication. It makes sense when you think about it. If we don't know how (and why) we come across as we do to others, and we don't know how to accurately read the nonverbals we get from others in a snap, then interactions — from small talk to office brainstorming sessions, let alone first dates, networking, and job interviews — can seem scary and mysterious.

The solution for this kind of social anxiety is the knowledge and self-confidence that I trust you are gaining as you read this book.

Second-Stage Impressions

A woman I know loves to tell a story about when she met her husband and how she and her mother differed in their opinions. Karen's husband, Matt, is a highly gregarious guy. He talks a lot and tends to be a little louder than most, especially when in a crowd. When he talks, his body moves, his arms flailing all over the place, putting emphasis on his words. When Karen met him, he had a devil-may-care attitude that was, in its way, charming. Matt didn't worry too much about how neat his hair was, or whether his clothes were clean or torn. Karen fell for him quickly, treasuring his individuality and his ability to make people laugh. When her boyfriend and other friends were over at her house, her new boyfriend tended to be the life of the party, and his voice could be heard throughout the house.

Karen's mom valued order and, to a great extent, quiet. About three months into the relationship, Karen noticed that her mom didn't join the conversation when it involved anything about Matt. One day, Karen confronted her mother. "Do you have a problem with Matt?" Karen asked.

"I don't know what you see in him or how you can care about him. He has no self-respect. He doesn't care about the way he looks, doesn't care about whether his clothes are clean, and he's obnoxious," her mom replied.

"Obnoxious?" Karen asked. "When has he ever been obnoxious to you or Dad?

"He hasn't been obnoxious to me in particular, but listen to how loud he is. Can't he control his volume? I'm not deaf, you know." Her mom also felt that Matt spent too much time talking to other people and didn't pay enough attention to Karen. The thought had never occurred to Karen; in fact, Karen loved everything her mom hated about Matt.

What you see when you encounter another person may differ from what someone else notices. After the first ninety seconds of interacting with someone, what we look for may be related to what we value. We begin to make associations between the non-verbal behaviors we witness and the inner qualities we believe they reflect. Then we separate the people we want to continue to interact with from those we don't. In this second-stage assessment, we filter everything we see and hear through our own personal experiences and biases and assign a type — that is, a stereotype — to them. A New Yorker's filter of experiences of a southerner's voice may create a stereotype that says southerners are slow. A southerner's filter of experiences may create a stereotype that says northerners are rude. *Studies show that the longer you consciously deliberate using those preferences to judge others, the less accurate and predictive they become.*

Ask yourself what you believe to be the most important quality another person can have. What characteristic or kind of personality do you value above all others? Think about it and write it down now. Now write down the second and third most important qualities.

Having done this exercise with thousands of people over the years, I have been amazed at the similarity of the answers among very different groups of people. From police officers to accountants, teachers to engineers, college students to executives, the answers are the same. The number one answer is usually "trustworthy," "real," "sincere," or "honest." Or people respond with phrases such as "they are just what you see" and "nothing phony." This makes sense, since all these are the characteristics that we, at the gut level, associate with another person's harmlessness and predictability.

The number two answer is usually "kind," "considerate," "polite," or "sensitive" — values that, again, indicate that someone is safe to be around. And the number three answer is usually "predictable," "reliable," "someone you can count on," or some other, related word or idea. People ask themselves, "Can I trust him? Does she care? Can I count on him?"

Some of the answers differ by gender. Women often say they value a good sense of humor, someone who laughs easily; men often say they look for someone who has a firm handshake or is confident and well groomed. Other answers are highly personal, such as "a good listener" or "someone who likes children." These values relate to the four factors that most affect our impressions of others: credibility, likability, attractiveness, and power.

To hone your skills, pay attention to your first gut-level impressions and your second-stage impressions. If you talk to someone new on the phone, write down some thoughts about her. If you meet someone and exchange contact information, record your impressions of him. If you exchange business cards, you can write down your first impression of him on the back. Go back to your impressions later and check for accuracy.

You'll notice as you begin to check for accuracy how your value system affects what you see in other people at that second stage of assessment. Whatever you hold as important will act as a filter in your judgment of others. For example, the first thing you may notice about a person is whether she's sincere. If you are talking to someone who does not make full eye contact, who has her head turned toward you but not her heart, whose words sound nice and gooey but whose nonverbal behaviors suggest that she is closed off, you may perceive her as not being "real." You may place her in the "be careful" category. Then you may begin to investigate what she might be hiding.

Though you may first pick up some of a person's behaviors in a snap impression, you may also consciously filter your impression through stereotypes. While sitting at a banquet table at an association event, I watched the former association president pick up my iced tea glass and begin drinking. I thought, "Oh, that's sweet. He didn't notice the glass was mine." His mistake actually humbled him and endeared him to me. To his right sat a professional speaker on business etiquette. She said to him, "You just drank from Patti's glass!" She later told me how appalled she was at his bad manners, and that a person of his stature should know that beverages sit to your right.

These differing reactions illustrate that personal factors affect how we assess someone else's behavior. My first impression of the man was that he was real and likable. I thought, "He's just an ordinary person like me." The woman who sat on his other side thought he was a complete oaf. I valued him for being real; she valued proper etiquette. Both values are valid, but they led to different impressions. Unlike the primal hardwiring that informs our snaps, our values are formed in our cognitive brains, and we base them on cultural and social factors. That means these second-stage impressions can be inaccurate and affected by stereotypes and prejudice, so be wary.

According to a 1982 study by Don E. Hamachek, three principles most affect second-stage impressions:

- We tend to give more weight to negative information than to positive information. My colleague ignored all

---

Your Actions Speak Louder Than Your Words

Match.com knows that you have values and desires that you are unaware of consciously but that you act on. The company uses algorithms that track what you look at on the Internet. As with the algorithms used by Amazon and Netflix to suggest products based on what you have viewed or purchased previously, Match .com's algorithms track the profiles you look at and the people you contact. You may say, "I want a Hindu-classical-music lover," but if the algorithms instead indicate that you actually look at and/or contact country music–loving hotties, the site views your behaviors as a better indication of what you will like in a partner. Match.com uses these to give you a "daily pick."

the president's positive cues — his warm smile, his gentle voice, and the way he would lean forward and make eye contact while listening to another person. She only saw the broken etiquette rule.

- We tend to be influenced by what's most obvious — drinking out of the wrong glass was pretty obvious.
- We tend to judge others on the assumption that most people are like us, or *should* be like us. My colleague would never break a rule of etiquette, and she expected others to be the same way.[2]

As you can see, both your stated values and your subconscious values affect the way you read people. And your impressions of others say as much about you as they do about the people you're assessing.

EXERCISE

Are You Like Me?

To see how your values affect the way you read people, record your first impressions of the next three people you meet either in person or over the phone.

1. List your impressions of the person — such as *harsh, friendly, cold, rich,* or *smart* — in one or two words or phrases. For example:
   Impression: Stuck-up. What's this person trying to prove?
2. Next, note as many of the person's nonverbal cues as you can, including clothing and artifacts (or accessories), facial expressions, voice, body, gestures, and so on. For example:
   Nonverbal Cues: Chin in the air, doesn't look at anybody, mouth tight and lips pursed, one hand

on the hip and the other holding a large, expensive purse and a large Starbucks coffee.

3. Write whether, based on the above, you view the person as like you or not like you, and briefly state why. For example:
    Like Me or Not: Not like me. I wouldn't dress or act like that.

4. Now analyze your data by answering these questions about your past experiences:

    *   Who have you met in your life that you immediately liked? What nonverbal cues did you pick up from this person that led you to like him or her? How accurate was your first impression?

    *   Who have you met in your life that you immediately disliked or didn't trust? What nonverbal cue did you pick up from this person that led you to dislike him or her? How accurate was your first impression?

(For an online version and examples go to "Are You Like Me?" at www.snapfirstimpressions.com.)

Initial encounters create an emotionally concentrated head-to-toe snapshot image that we use to assess thousands of cues in an instant. This snap is highly accurate and lasting, but assumptions based on stereotypes are not. Such assumptions group people into broad categories based on a lack of commonalities — he is not like me, which I can perceive through easily readable information like skin color or age.

Research says we typically assign more negative behaviors to people we have stereotyped, so we give them less conversation time, less eye contact, fewer smiles, and so on. This is unfortunate, as one of the few ways of changing a first impression is to see that person in other contexts.

Improving the Snap Impression You Make

A group of friends gathered for a monthly dinner party hosted by Scott and Julie. Julie's friend Debbie happened to drop by and was introduced to everyone, after which she stayed for dinner.

Debbie sat at the head of the table and proceeded to talk about herself for the entire dinner. People were exchanging raised eyebrows and grimaces. Several people tried to start conversations that everyone could join in, but Debbie just jumped over them like a rabbit, talking louder and faster.

I was at this dinner and observed Debbie's behavior. I realized about halfway through the dinner that I was annoyed with Debbie because I couldn't talk and because her behavior reminded me of my own tendency to overtalk. Debbie was my "yuck mirror." Throughout my life I have met people and thought, "Yuck!" Usually, I've later realized that what annoyed me about them was a quality I fear or battle in myself.

To give yourself a second chance at making a good impression, and as you work on reading your first impressions of others, notice if you dislike someone at first sight or are irked by a behavior in anyone. Then be polite and use the yuck mirror to improve yourself. Here are some questions to help you do this:

- What's the behavior I don't like?
- Did I ever have this behavior?
- How can I have empathy for that person?
- Is he or she like me in some way?
- How can I use this mirror to improve my behavior?
- What action can I take to change the behavior?

In my "Effective Executive Meetings" and "First Impressions and Etiquette for the Sales Professional" programs, I use the insight that Debbie provided me. Here are the key things to consider.

1. Ask yourself whose voice you hear most when you're with other people. If it's yours, you are talking too much.

You may be a rabbit. (See chapter 5 for the definition.) If you answered, "I don't hear my voice, but I wish I could be part of the conversation," then you may be a turtle.

2. If you are a rabbit, practice being silent, or asking questions and listening. If you are a turtle, practice stating a topic and your perspective on it, and then ask the other person to answer a question. (Because I am naturally curious, and would love to have my own talk show so that I could ask fun questions, my snap change is to practice asking questions and then *gently* listening.)

3. Ask a question that starts an interesting conversation for everyone. If you answer the question, do so briefly. If you're a rabbit, you may want to wait until everyone else has had a chance.

Good Conversation Starters

When you see or read something interesting, scan it or make note of it. You might even list these conversation starters in a file on your smartphone or tablet. I've found the following questions effective:

- What's the best thing that happened in your life in the past year?
- What's the most enjoyable thing you have done in the past week?
- What's one thing you would try to change about _____ [fill in the blank with a current event in the news]?
- What is the best thing about _____ [fill in the blank with the other person's line of work]? Or: What is something new for you at work?
- We all have favorite foods, but if you were offered only three foods on a fork that contained the last bites of your life, what three foods would be on the fork?

Try using some of these questions in the next twenty-four hours. Watch how you ask the questions, and notice the nonverbal snaps of people as they answer.

8. WORK WORLD SNAPS

Shine in Interviews, Sales Calls, Meetings, Presentations, and Negotiations

A recent coaching client of mine was anxious about an up-coming job interview, and his stress was evident in his body language. He was holding his hands in his lap and had his feet tucked under the chair. His voice was so soft that I continually had to ask him to repeat his statement. I asked him what he wanted his interviewer to feel about him. He told me he wanted the interviewer to feel excitement. So I asked my client to imagine how he behaved when he was excited. Then I asked him to act that way. His body language and paralanguage changed immediately. He held his head and torso up, leaned forward, and gestured up and out. He used an energy-charged voice to share his positive work experiences. He smiled and even laughed as he relayed one particular story. But he hadn't felt excited before he started moving his body. "As soon as I brought my shoulders back and smiled, and put some energy in my voice," he said, "I got genuinely excited."

Today, with so many people looking for work or anxious to keep the work they have, I'd like to help you use body language and first impressions to your best advantage. We'll look closely at job interviews — with all their potential stressors — but the tips also apply to interactions that can occur in many other instances where you meet others face-to-face, such as sales calls, customer and client meetings, presentations, and negotiations. Even if you are not interviewing for a job, the insights you'll find in this chapter will help you improve the impression you make and your access to others.

I've discussed some of these insights and research in previous chapters; my goal here is to guide you step-by-step as you learn how to put them into *action* in real-life situations. As always, begin every interview, sales call, and client or customer presentation or negotiation without judgment and with the sincere desire to understand and connect.

Tips for Looking Great in an Interview or Other First Meeting

It's essential to understand how important snap impressions are. Hiring decisions are often made within the first ten seconds of the interview, sometimes before you even formally begin the conversation. Remember, we're able to read up to ten thousand nonverbal cues in less than a minute. When we talk about getting a gut feeling about a person, what we're really talking about is reading all those nonverbal cues *very* quickly. Many hiring decisions in interviews are based on reading those cues in an instinctual way, with the interviewer then spending the rest of the interview looking for evidence to back up her initial snap.

Let's take a detailed look at what you can do to give your best snap in an interview. It's easy to lose sight of these basics when you have a lot on your mind — and a lot on the line. But they matter. This is a section to come back to before an important first meeting. It also might be a section that you discuss in your place of business or with your clients to see what small details they noticed that affected their first impressions.

Rehearse Success, Merge, and Pop

Use these three tools to improve the first impression you make on your interviewer.

Rehearse success: Visualize your success before the interview, rather than imagining all the things you might do wrong. Prepare by first practicing "live" and then closing your eyes and visualizing yourself in the situation. Imagine how you will shake hands well and sit with confidence, be warm and friendly, listen attentively and answer with confidence all the questions you're asked. Play the movie of you giving a successful interview in your head over and over so that when you are under stress, you can easily go to the positive, successful responses you have rehearsed. (Go to www.snapfirstimpressions.com for an audio download that will take you through a relaxation exercise, and for my vocal guide to this positive visualization.)

Merge: In my work with the client whose story begins this chapter, I used an exercise called merging. I asked him to think of times on the job, or in his personal life, when he experienced a success, an emotionally satisfying experience. We create and experience stories in the emotional right hemisphere of our brain. When we recall and retell these stories, we reexperience the feelings that accompany them. By using the merging technique, you can bring positive emotions and success into any situation.

Pop: My client was having trouble visualizing success after a number of negative job interview experiences. He didn't have a positive memory of a work scenario to recall. We recorded the coaching session, and then we used what I call my pop tool, so he could "pop" to a more upbeat, optimistic attitude. This tool enables you to transfer the positive emotions you have felt in one situation to entirely different circumstances. Since my client wanted to appear energetic and confident, I asked him to recall what activities or situations made him feel that way. "Sailing!" he quickly replied, and his whole demeanor changed as he explained why. While he was in this mode, I asked him to "anchor" these feelings to his subconscious by briefly touching his leg. Then we watched our recording, and he touched his leg when he saw and felt the confidence and excitement he liked. In subsequent job interviews, he was able to "pop" to those emotions and nonverbals by briefly touching his leg.

Dress for Success

To prepare for a big interview, Madeline picked out a conservative pinstriped jacket and skirt that she had recently purchased on sale. She carefully clipped off all the tags and checked out the fit in front of her mirror. On her interview day, she shook hands with her interviewer, a man in his forties with gray sideburns. During their conversation, Madeline noticed that "Mr. Gray" frequently tilted his head and body to her right side. Though she thought it was odd, she didn't mention it, assuming he had a bad back and was trying to make himself comfortable. When she got into her car, she realized that the side seam in her new skirt had come apart — revealing more of her in her interview than she had intended! Lesson: Don't just try on your interview outfit. Move around in it, sit and stand in it, even consider having a friend take a picture of you wearing it. And by all means, check the seams.

In an interview, you are dressing to show respect for the company and the interviewer. The culture of the company you are interviewing with matters. The general guideline is to dress one or two levels up from whatever would be appropriate for

the day-to-day work environment in that particular office,
and no more than two levels
down or up from the interviewer's status. (Go to www.snapfirst
impressions.com for a discussion of these levels.) If you are
older and you overdress for an
interview, your employer may
interpret that as your being
out of touch with the current
culture in other ways. Keep in
mind that it is perfectly okay to
ask in advance what the appropriate attire would be for the
interview. You can incorporate
this question into initial conversations or emails with the
interviewer, along with other
inquiries such as a request for
directions to the office.

> **Stress-Reduction Tip**
>
> The mistake I see most often takes place in the first essential moments of an interview. Sometimes you're so focused on you (on your nerves, how you look, and so on) that you're not doing what you would do naturally: focus on the other person. Making a connection with the interviewer should be uppermost in your mind and the main focus of your actions. Your most important goal in any interaction is to make the other person feel comfortable. By doing so you're no longer focused on yourself and your fears. The added benefit: research on self-focused or other-focused interviewees shows that the other-focused interviewees received higher ratings and got more job offers.

Strive to be fashion current in colors, style, and jewelry, including your watch. If you aren't sure what is current in professional clothing, read an appropriate men or women's style
magazine or go to a high-end clothing or department store and
look around.

Show You Came Prepared

While you don't want to be overburdened with stuff, don't come
empty-handed, either. Old-school interviewers will expect you
to bring a nice, perhaps leather-bound, notebook with a pad
and pen clipped inside. The pocket should have copies of your
résumé and the printed-out Internet research you did on the

company and the job. You can even pull out the research you did on the company and ask the interviewer a question you have prepared based on your research.

You might prefer to bring your new high-tech smartphone or tablet, but remember that we like people who are like us. The technology or lack of it should match that of the company, the job, and the interviewer. It can be awkward if the interviewer does not have the same technology you have, and it might be easy for you to become distracted and glance at your gadgetry, which may give the interviewer the impression that you are more interested in it than in talking to her. In the same way, if your interview is with a high-tech company or your interviewer is under thirty, bring your latest and greatest gadget to match her techno impression.

Greet with Feeling, Not Your Stuff

What if you're sitting and somebody comes out to greet you? Don't do what most people do first: pick up all your things. Instead, leave your stuff where it is and stand up to greet your interviewer. Shake hands. Make eye contact. Connect with that person. Then pick up your belongings and follow your interviewer into the office. And if you are meeting in someone's office, don't plop all your stuff down on his desk.

Ditch the Stuff to Look More Powerful

I walked into a television studio to do an interview alongside another guest. I had my coat, purse, and notes in hand, while my savvy fellow guest carried only his confidence. I fluttered like a bird, trying to arrange my stuff on a side table. When I got to the interview chair, I fluttered some more, arranging my heels, hair, and jewelry. In the midst of all this moving about, I realized I would have looked — and felt — more confident if I'd left my purse and coat in the car, instead of worrying and fluttering, and had calmly glided into my seat.

Research bears this out. Women's clothing, and our accessories like shoes and handbags, affect our power. We make sixteen to sixty distinct body language movements as we move toward a chair and sit down; men make three to fourteen.

Be Polite Verbally and Nonverbally

The smallest things you do and say count. They can show that you are caring and courteous. For example, hold the door for the interviewer if it's appropriate. If she doesn't ask you to take a seat first, wait for her to take hers before you sit. At the beginning of the interview, and again at the end of the interview, thank her for taking the time to speak with you.

In addressing your interviewer, it's always best to mirror her level of formality. If you're interviewing straight out of college, or anytime you're in doubt about the proper level of formality, err on the side of formality and use "Mr." or "Ms." and the interviewer's last name, at least initially. Then follow the interviewer's lead.

How Formally Should I Behave?

The status level of the other person should guide your conduct throughout the meeting. Clients have asked me if it is ever acceptable to share jokes or personal anecdotes if the interviewer does so. That depends on the status level of the interviewer. Will she be your boss, or is this person a human resources person? The level of formality will also be directed by the individual interviewer's personality. But in general, don't go to extremes on either end.

One human resources person shared this with me: "I certainly appreciate and hire people who are comfortable but not disrespectful. Many times, though, I have had job candidates who obviously thought their interviews were going very well, because they were laughing and telling stories. But it was clear to me that they weren't in touch with my demeanor, because I was uncomfortable and thought they were far too chummy."

Make Eye Contact

As I mentioned earlier, in typical conversation you're making eye contact about 60 percent of the time. But it's also important to realize that it is normal to look away from time to time as you speak, because you're accessing information in your brain. Actually, the listener should be the one making the most eye contact. So when your interviewer is talking, you're locked in. Keeping the eye connection tells the interviewer you are paying attention and are interested in the job. After giving an answer, remember to make eye contact and listen to the interviewer; don't click off when you are not on. Eye contact sends the message that you are serious and engaged.

Where'd They Go?

Your interviewer may back away from you, break off eye contact, or stop giving you nonverbal feedback. If you're sensing that something has shifted or changed, don't freak out. Keep being yourself: listening, connecting, and answering the interviewer's questions. If it's appropriate and fits your personality, you can even choose to be a bit feisty and say, "What can I do right now to convince you that I'd be the best person for this job?"

Lean into It

Leaning forward shows that you are interested and listening. You can lean forward with your head, your upper torso, or your whole body to show you are connecting to what the interviewer is saying. But don't overdo it; you're not trying to "get in their face." Just aim for gentle, timely leans. As interviewees, we tend to pull back when we don't like or are fearful of a question. Making an effort to move forward shows the interviewer you're focused on her and not on yourself.

EXERCISE

Breath Tool for Calmness and Confidence

When you get upset or nervous, notice your breathing. Right now, look at your watch, cell phone, or clock and count the number of times you breathe in and out in a minute. You may notice that even at rest your breathing is faster than the "average" rate of twelve to fourteen times a minute (a rate that is already faster than it needs to be). In fact, many of us, without knowing it, habitually hyperventilate — that is, we take quick, shallow breaths from the top of the chest. This kind of breathing sharply reduces the level of carbon dioxide in our blood. This reduced level of carbon dioxide causes the arteries, including the carotid artery going to the brain, to constrict, thus reducing the flow of blood throughout the body. When this occurs, no matter how much oxygen you may breathe into your lungs, your brain and body will experience a shortage of oxygen. The lack of oxygen switches on the sympathetic nervous system — our freeze-flight-fight-or-faint reflex. That reflex enabled our ancestors to freeze so they wouldn't be seen by, or to flee from, or, if necessary, to fight something like a saber-toothed tiger, but now it just makes us tense, anxious, and irritable.

When you take quick shallow breaths, you reduce your ability to think clearly. During a job interview, this may keep you from answering questions quickly and succinctly. One key to feeling clearheaded, energized, and confident is to breathe deeply, from low down in your belly. Practice breathing more slowly using your diaphragm, belly, rib cage, and lower back in the process. It's amazing how strong and powerful you feel when you take deep belly breaths, letting the air fill you up, and letting out that breath fully and completely in deep, releasing sighs. Of course, you aren't going to be doing this type of breathing *during* an interview, but try it whenever you get anxious and certainly before your interview.

Try it right now. Take in four deep belly breaths on a count of four, hold for a count of two, and make lots of noise as you deeply sigh out all your breath.

Speak with Strength

Everyone, but especially women, should be sure that their voices stay strong until the end of each sentence. Women's voices tend to go up at the end of a sentence, as if they're asking a question instead of making a definitive statement. That makes them sound as if they don't trust themselves, which can leave a bad impression. You want to sound confident. Practice answering questions with a strong voice, and even record yourself as you practice if you know you have a tendency to lilt.

(Go to "Snap Gender Differences" at my website, www.snap firstimpressions.com, to hear high and low sentence endings by both men and women as they speak during interviews, sales presentations, and negotiations. Notice which ones convey confidence.)

How to Sit

Be big and open. When you're afraid, your body retracts and gets smaller. This makes sense because, if you are afraid of being attacked, it's smart to try to make yourself smaller or invisible. But in a job interview, no matter how you feel when you start, act brave with your body language and keep your body open. As I described in the true story that opens this chapter, the body sends messages to the brain. Within seconds of adopting a brave, open stance, you'll begin to *feel* more confident and brave.

Don't take up significantly more space than the interviewer if he is in a position of authority. Be careful how you sit in a chair. Research says that women perch, sitting on the edge of the seat, arching their backs, while men tend to slouch, relying more on the backrest. Perching the entire time makes you look less powerful. Vary your position, use lots of space, and put your arms on the armrest to look confident. As your mother told you, don't slouch. I have to be careful because of my curved spine, so I compensate with big gestures. If you slouch, you may look old and tired rather than vital and energetic. Sit forward slowly as you share information you're confident in.

Show Your Hand(s)

Don't hide your hands under the table or in your pockets or otherwise tuck them away. Keep your hands open and in view on the table or the arms of the chair. Gesture normally. If you are extremely nervous, you can briefly hold your own hand to comfort yourself, but only briefly. Your hands show your emotional state. When you close your hand, the amount of tightness and the way the fingers curve show how you feel about the topic being discussed and the person you are with. In an interview, you want to be open, not closed.

Match and Mirror

We like people who are like us, and research shows that interviewers tend to hire people who are like them. So match and mirror your interviewer enough at the beginning of the interview to make him comfortable with you. You might lean slightly in the direction he is leaning, for instance, or match his smile with one of your own.

Stay Up

Remember, when we're in an upbeat mood, our gestures move up, our head comes up, our shoulders come up and back, and even our feet seem to lift in a lighter, bouncier way. Not quite like Tigger in Winnie the Pooh, but in a way that directs your energy upward. Before a job interview or any stressful meeting, work on yourself "from the outside in" to change your mood and behavior by doing things that make you feel positive inside. Talk to a friend, watch something funny, or listen to music that makes you sing along in your car on the way to the meeting.

Get Grounded

When people are nervous, they tend to either move a lot or freeze. Here's a trick: when you're in the thick of the most difficult questions and want to achieve the highest levels of cognition, place both feet firmly on the ground. This placement actually makes it easier to utilize both hemispheres of the brain — the rational and the creative-emotional. Or, if you feel yourself freeze, move your feet in some way.

End Well

Remember the recency effect? The last thing you say or do tends to matter a great deal. So as the conversation winds down, make sure your belongings are on the left side of your body so you can easily shake with your right hand. You may shake hands more than once — when you get up, at the door, and after talking for a bit longer while parting. Make that seem like the most natural thing in the world, because every time you shake hands, you're bonding. Even if you feel you didn't do as well as you would have liked in the interview, you can improve the impression you make by closing strongly and confidently. Some people turn off when they feel they haven't nailed it. Instead, stay present and poised all the way to the end.

Choose Confidence

We don't want to appear arrogant in an interview, but we do want to come across as sure of ourselves and our qualifications. To express that kind of confidence via your body language, put your body in an open position, with your arms away from your body, legs uncrossed, and shoulders down and back. Keep your heart window forward, extend eye contact for as long as three seconds, and let your voice descend slightly at the end of your sentences.

Avoid Overconfidence

Mark was excited about his interview for a summer job at a bank. He thought the interview was in the bag since his dad was a good friend of the bank manager, Bob. The interview day dawned sunny and warm, so Mark planned to hit the waves and surf after the interview. He even put his swim trunks on under his Calvin Klein suit. After the interview, Mark was pumped, thinking he had rocked! He went out to his car in the parking lot of a store next to the bank, opened the back, and stripped out of his business suit and down to his bathing trunks. He put on a T-shirt, hung his suit in the back of the car, and drove off singing the old Beach Boys hit "Surfin' USA." He didn't notice that Bob's office looked out at that same parking lot, and that his interviewer had just gotten a view of his quick-change shenanigans.

Bob called Mark's dad and told him the strip story. But that wasn't the only problem. He added, "I have to tell you that when your son came in today, he held his chin up high and smirked as he shook my hand. He seemed to think the interview was just a formality, and I got a bad first impression."

Pause and Reflect

After your interview, take a few moments to debrief and write down your impression of how it went. Think of what you did well, and pat yourself on the back. Note any questions you feel you didn't answer well. Consider a positive moment you might mention in your follow-up thank you. Completing a job interview is like climbing a mountain, so sit back a moment and congratulate yourself. (More interview tips and a comprehensive interview debriefing sheet are available at www.snap firstimpressions.com.) Send a thank-you. An email of thanks can be sent immediately after the interview, but good etiquette and good job offers warrant a hard-mail thank-you note later. (For five tips for writing great thank-you notes, and for sample thank-you notes, go to www.snapfirstimpressions.com.)

How Are You Coming Across to Others?

During a job interview — or business meeting or sales call — wouldn't it be great if you could read the other person's mind? You can almost do that by reading her body language, which can reflect the following states of mind.

Confusion: When a person is confused, she may move in a random way, picking things up and putting them down, shifting in her seat, or shuffling her feet. Her brow may furrow, and she may rub her eyes or face, typically downward, as if she wants to clear her head of confusion. She may touch her temple or forehead, symbolically pushing the "on" button of her brain. Her eyes may blink open and closed, as if she hopes that this will help her see more clearly. If you get these cues, succinctly clarify your message and ask if your listener has any questions.

Fatigue or boredom: When someone has shut down or turned off, he may turn away from you or slump in his seat. He might lean backward and lazily rest his arm on the back of a chair or sofa. He might also pantomime "nap time" by slumping forward and, to some degree, lying across the table! Or he may simply break eye contact, fix his gaze in space, and close his eyes for periods. For whatever reason — a reason that may have nothing to do with you — this person is no longer tuned in.

Impatience: If your listener is checking her watch or PDA, she is anxious to wrap up. She may subconsciously do something with her feet to indicate she is "on her way out" — something like tapping her foot.

Suspicion: When someone is suspicious of you or of what you are saying, he will look like a judge trying to form an opinion. He is apt to look uncomfortable, with a furrowed brow, squinting eyes, and downward glances. He may tighten his lips as though to squelch a negative comment.

As I've said, body language is supremely symbolic. So, if someone rubs her nose, eyes, or ear, she may be trying to tell you that what you are saying doesn't smell, look, or sound right to her. This is a cue to emphasize your credibility.

Excitement or happiness: On the more positive side, when the other person is excited by what you are saying or happy with your response, he will reflect those good feelings. Look for shifts upward in face, body, and voice. You might see him inhale deeply, shift his weight, or rock forward in his seat. A person will signal his interest by smiling, tilting his head in the direction of hearing you better, leaning forward, and furrowing his brow — with interest. This means you are on the right track. Good job!

Tips for Conducting an Interview

When you are the one doing the interviewing, remember that we form impressions — and tend to hire — according to a candidate's social skills. Of course we think we are right in our hiring decisions, but we also tend to like, and thus hire, people who are like us. The traits that get someone the job may not be the traits needed to do the job.

Whether you are a human resources professional hiring for your company, a business owner looking for a new customer service person, or a manager interviewing a job candidate or doing a performance appraisal, you can use the following tips as a checklist for your next interview.

1. Be prepared. Many interviewers spend only a minute or two looking at a résumé to prepare for an interview. Have in mind the following three details.

    - What you're looking for in an employee.
    - Your first three questions.
    - What you will say and do when closing the interview. Your preparation affects not only the interview but also the job seeker's impression of your organization.

2. Be on time. Don't make interviewees wait and sweat. Candidates say 48 percent of interviewers come in late or otherwise make them wait.

3. Have an open attitude. According to research, 54 percent of interviewers admit they have taken an instant dislike to a candidate. You want an accurate snap, not a stereotype. Research says that, contrary to lay wisdom, highly trusting interviewers are significantly better than others at detecting lies.

4. Stay open and attentive. Keep your body windows open and watch your feet.

5. Create a natural back-and-forth conversation. Fifty-one percent of candidates feel as if they are being cross-examined or interrogated.

6. Listen more and talk less. According to interview coach Carole Martin, the candidate should talk 80 percent of the time, the interviewer 20 percent. Halfway through

the interview session, check out the flow. It may help your listening ability and your memory to take notes.

7. Remember the candidate's name. Thirty percent of candidates say their interviewers did not remember their names. You can even create cards or name tents (place cards) to help you remember the candidate's name and the candidate to remember yours.

8. Take your time. When you are stressed and/or the candidate is, you may naturally want to rush through the process in a flight response. Breathe, take breaks, and put a reminder note in front of you to slow down. If you are a rabbit interviewing a turtle, make sure you allow ten seconds of silence after you ask a question. Watch that you don't just jump in to speed things up. Candidates say that 70 percent of interviewers act as if there's no time to talk.

9. Smile. This makes you look welcoming — and less like a judge and jury.[1]

10. Take the candidate to the door and make sure to leave a good last impression.

9. YOUR SOCIAL SNAP

Be Confident and Attract What You Want While Dating, Socializing, and Networking

Two women were at a museum gathering: Suni, a short brunette, and her tall blonde friend. Suni spied a tall, dark, handsome stranger across the room. They smiled and he approached her, accompanied by his shorter blond male friend. Suni, being short, knew she was likely to be more appealing to the blond guy and she thought, "He is handsome, too, but I want the tall one. I am going to use matching and mirroring to signal to the tall guy that I like him." As the tall one leaned to the side, tilted his head, and put his hand on his hip, Suni mirrored each action, including the tone and pitch of his voice. When he leaned forward and smiled, Suni leaned forward. They "danced" with their movements. She was smitten, so her moves were motivated by an authentic feeling. Sure enough, the tall one asked Suni for her business card, much to the chagrin of his short friend.

Suni found out much later that the shorter one had whispered to his pal as they had approached her, "I'm interested in the little brunette." But after talking with her, the taller one came to feel that he and Suni were such a good

*match that he had to ask her out himself. A year later, she is
still dating him, and thinks that matching is pretty powerful
stuff!*

In the above story, Suni matched the tall guy's body movements and his paralanguage. It's also helpful to match someone's breathing. When we are completely relaxed, we breathe
down deep in the belly, just as babies do. This breathing allows
us to take very full breaths and completely fill up our lungs and
exhale all the carbon dioxide. When we're neither completely
relaxed nor tense, we breathe from the midchest area, and when
we're nervous or tense, we breathe faster and high in the chest,
above the heart level. Obviously, matching someone's breath
can really tune you in to that person.

The mate-selection process is something that operates at
an instinctual, unconscious level. But if that's true, then why
is it that we sometimes have such difficulty in attracting the
attention of a man or woman who interests us? Often, we stifle
the natural body cues that let someone know we are approachable and interested. Fortunately, you can learn to "unstifle"
those cues and consciously change your body language to subtly invite attention. Matching or mirroring the object of your
affection, whether in actions or simply in your breathing, is one
way. There are many others.

So many of our body language cues are read and formed in
the limbic brain, where all the more primal instincts are located.
And, as we've seen, we form them quickly. In those first few seconds, we aren't exchanging a lot of words; we are exchanging a
lot of nonverbal communication, most of it subconsciously. To
attract the right person, you need to bring some of that subconscious knowledge up to your conscious control.

Men and women need to do different things to make themselves approachable, attractive, and available to people they're

romantically interested in. You need to know the signals to send and which signals to look for from the other person.

Seven Signals That Make
a Woman Approachable

If you are a single woman at a networking event, sitting at a sports bar, or sipping coffee at a café, men are all over the place. You're intelligent and self-confident, and you're ready, willing, and able to date, but it's hard to get men to approach. Other than imagining they are big ole bears and slathering yourself with honey, how do you do it? If you are a single guy, what do you look for?

When you think of attraction and flirting, think like a caveman or -woman. Like our cave-dwelling ancestors, we are afraid of strangers. So we form first impressions quickly to decide whether it is safe to approach. As a woman, how do you get someone who doesn't know you to feel comfortable coming over to talk in a public setting, or to start a conversation with you at a dinner party? How do you get him to pick you out of the group? How do you tell someone things about you without words? Let your body do the talking.

First, to make yourself more approachable, give off "harmlessness" cues. In dating, you want to make yourself appear safe and approachable. This may not be easy for you. Some of us have gotten so good at being independent, self-sufficient, and powerful that, in a first encounter, we forget we might scare men off, even strong and confident men. What is great for women in business can be off-putting in the attraction phase of romantic socializing. Remember that the soft, vulnerable part of you that you have been so good at protecting in business is actually appealing in the flirting or dating process.

You might be thinking that you need to be natural. Actually, these *are* very natural movements. It's the bravado you use to cover up your true self that is unnatural and tends to put off or scare others away. So how can you hold and move your body to say, "I'm safe. I'm not going to bite"? I coach women to use the following seven signs of approachability. If you're a man, read these cues in order to recognize women who are showing you they are safe to talk to.

Don't Take Up Too Much Physical Space

This means don't spread your bag and jacket over all the chairs and take up the entire table with your paraphernalia at the coffee shop, and don't stand or sit with your legs too far apart. You learned in chapter 2 that taking up too much space communicates that you are powerful and superior. We want to show that we are strong women, but remember we are trying to get a man to come over and talk to us. You have to show you have room for someone else in your life.

Stand Slightly Pigeon-Toed

Men usually stand with their feet six to ten inches apart. Toes pointed inward or outward actually show your status in the hierarchy. Toes pointed outward say, "I'm mighty." Toes pointed inward say, "I'm approachable." Standing with your feet far apart with the toes out makes you look strong and actually signals that you could attack. Women usually stand with their feet four to six inches apart. To be very approachable, stand with your feet no more than six inches apart, and if you see someone nearby that you are particularly interested in and wish to have him feel comfortable coming over to you, point your toes *slightly* inward.

Walk This Way

If you take a close look at the way you walk in shoes, you might find that some of your shoes make you walk duck-footed, with your toes pointed outward. Toss those shoes. Walking with toes pointed outward is a "hands-off" signal. It is a walk often predicated by weight and pregnancy. Of course, pregnant women can be attractive, but for obvious reasons, single men rarely approach pregnant women to ask them out for drinks.

EXERCISE

Shoe Snaps

If you are a woman, walk in all your shoes, and notice how they affect your stance, your gait, and your posture. Ideally, do this in front of a mirror. Notice other women as they walk in different shoes. Flip-flops, clogs, and flat boots are comfortable, but they can also make you shuffle your feet and walk with your legs slightly wider apart and somewhat bowlegged at the thighs. Some shoes can make you hunch over or walk more like a man does, leading with a flat pelvis, rather than with a swing in the hips. High heels can make you swing your hips and take very appealing short steps, but if there is a grimace on your face that says, "I am in agony in these shoes," they don't help your approachability.

Smile

Okay, it's obvious, but when we're tense, we don't give a full open smile, and when we are trying to look cool we often don't smile at all. The smile is an international signal of friendliness. That's why the iconic smile-sneers on Jack Nicholson's face as he comes after the little boy in *The Shining*, and the Joker's face in the Batman movies, are so scary. They're not normal. Remember that a smile means safety, not danger. Have you ever had some guy ask you why you aren't smiling? That's because men feel more comfortable about approaching you when you're smiling.

Shrug

When turtles sense danger, they retreat by tucking their heads all the way into their shells. To protect our heads when we are startled, we pull our shoulders up toward our ears, and pull our heads and shoulders down and in. We shrug, bringing the shoulders up, and often tilt our heads and put out our upraised palms to say, "Hey, it's not my fault," or "I don't know," or "Whatever you want." A brief, small shrug accompanied by a glance at a man you're interested in tells him you are amenable. This doesn't signal that you're a pushover, just that you're approachable. I have seen women who are masters of the shoulder shrug. They make it look like a sensual feline move. They see a cute man, look at him briefly, then shrug. Right now, slowly lift your shoulders up and let them down. Try it a few times until you feel at ease with the motion.

Approachability and Men

If you are a man, some of the cues in the section "Seven Signals That Make a Woman Approachable" can be adapted to work for you. But many of these approachability cues can make you look less powerful. Alpha body language is often sexier. Remember, men are traditionally the hunters, the ones who approach. I know that women do approach men, but perhaps you should try making the first move yourself.

Tilt Your Head

The head tilt is not a uniquely feminine move, but it's certainly done more by women, as it's typically a signal of submission. A head tilt symbolically bares the neck. It mimics a head movement done by wolves when approached by the leader of the pack. This movement says, "I'm exposing my most vulnerable spot to you to show you I know you can rip me to pieces. So let's not fight about it." Head tilts are also nonverbal signals of intent listening. Imagine your ear tilted toward the speaker symbolically saying, "Pour more of what you're saying into me." Men tend to boast when they are flirting. They will talk a lot about what they have done and what they can do. In those initial conversations (or monologues), tilt your head to show you are listening. And by the way, boasting behavior is not an indication of whether a man will listen to you. If he's not listening now, it's only an indication that he wants your approval and admiration in that moment. For the man who reads this: if you don't see a woman tilt her head, she might not want you to talk more.

Uncross Your Arms

Finally, and as we've discussed in other contexts, uncross your arms. This opens up your heart window. Crossed arms can form a protective wall. It's pretty obvious that to get a man to approach you, you have to let the wall down — or at least lower the drawbridge. Holding a beverage in your hand will give you some security if you need that in order to uncross. Or if you're sitting at a coffeehouse, you can put your hands out in front of you on the table.

> **Come Hither, *Now!***
>
> For tips on signaling not just approachability but also your active interest, see "Luring Cues," as well as photos and videos of the moves, at www.snapfirstimpressions.com.

If you're still nervous, remember the "anchor" tool. Think of a time when you felt calm and confident, connect it to a slight, subtle motion such as briefly touching your leg or tummy, and then, when you're tense, use that motion to take you back to a calmer, more confident place.

How a Man Conveys Interest

Some of the following cues aren't gender-specific, since both males and females use them. It is important to note, however, that males and females can be very different in their snaps. Although this discussion is addressed mainly to women, if you're a man you can use these cues to signal your interest to a woman.

He lifts his eyebrows. When a man sees someone he's into, he automatically lifts and lowers his eyebrows, wrinkling his forehead in the process. But you'll have to keep your eyes peeled to catch a glimpse of this telltale signal. Anthropologists call it the eyebrow flash because, like a bolt of lightning in the night sky, it moves across the face quickly.

He stands with his legs spread apart. Men want to show themselves at their alpha-male, leader-of-the-pack best. A guy will often stand with his legs spread apart and pelvis facing you when he's attracted to you. It's a primal, biological instinct, and most men don't even know they're doing it.

He stands or sits with his toes pointed toward each other. This means he's feeling a little unsure of himself; he's interested but needs reassurance that the interest is mutual.

He tilts his head slightly to the side when your eyes meet. Just as it is for a woman, the head tilt is a subconscious come-hither signal that the guy is attracted to you. So if the man you've been sharing glances with gives you the head tilt, that's your cue he is interested but possibly a bit shy.

Danger/Attraction at First Sight

While our snap assessments of other people may be very clear indicators of who is safe to like or dislike, we may still get into trouble when attraction is involved. You see a man across the room and everything in your body screams "Danger!" And yet you have to have him. This is what happened to my pal Maddison. "I first saw him at a party at a friend's house," she told me. "He was staring at me, not blinking, like I was an ice cream cone. That, his leather jacket, and thumb locked over jeans at the zipper made me shiver. My first impression: 'This guy is dangerous.' My second thought: 'I want him.' I should have paid attention to my first impression. As he walked toward me, my heart was beating so fast that I stepped back and tried to turn away. My body was trying to run, but I didn't. By the end of the night I was a goner.

"He was incredibly sexy and a wonderful kisser, but after a few months, one of the guys in our gang of mutual friends called me up. He told me what everyone else knew: my lust object was dangerous. He was sleeping with lots of other women. This hurt like heck, but I did learn that my first impression — 'This guy is dangerous' — had been accurate, which is good to know. It'll be useful the next time around."

Attraction can override the self-protective first impression in a heartbeat. Attraction — when your blood pressure goes up, your heart races, and your palms sweat — mimics the freeze-flight-fight-or-faint response associated with fear. Scariness is strangely exciting. That's why we go to horror movies. You just shouldn't *date* them.

As I discussed in chapter 2, a charismatic person who chooses to lie can get away with it more easily. In dating, you need to be especially aware of this. When you're highly attracted to someone you've just met, do a check-in on credibility and make sure you're feeling a pull toward True North.

Eight Tips for Social Events and Networking

You may jump for joy when you think of social gatherings, while others hear "wine and cheese" or "punch and cookies" and start to feel their palms sweat and stomachs churn. If you're in the latter group, here are eight tips to make mingling and meeting new people more comfortable, successful, and even fun.

Go Early Rather Than Late

If you get there before other guests, it's easier to get acclimated. You can stand with the host if you need courage or introductions. You can even ask for an anxiety-distracting task like taking coats from new arrivals or asking if they would like a drink. Nervousness comes out of your body in many ways. One way is through your hands. When your hands are confidently occupied with useful tasks, that confidence message goes to your brain and affects your entire body. It also gives you an easily repeatable script. Questions such as "Would you like me to take your coat?" and "What can I get you to drink?" open conversation.

Stand Near the Best-Smelling Food

This may sound strange, but research has actually shown that this is where people gravitate, and that pleasant aromas give rise to pleasant mood states. What's more, persuasion research shows that when we feel good, we associate those pleasant feelings with the people we are with. This is why, when I speak to real estate professionals, I often recommend that they advise home sellers to bake a batch of chocolate chip cookies or a loaf of bread, or to sauté onions in butter, before an open house. These smells are shown to create positive feelings — and to positively influence visitors' view of the house. If you are a single woman, stand near the cheese and salami to meet men, and near cinnamon buns if you want a man to kiss you. Research on olfaction says the smell of cinnamon is arousing for men. (I am thinking of creating my own cologne!)

Use Your Hands

Food gives you an easy conversation opener — "Have you tried the crab dip? It's great." And, like taking coats, the act of holding out plates, spooning up portions, or pouring out drinks gives you something to do with your hands. When you're nervous, you may want to hide your hands in your pockets or give yourself a comfort cue and rub your ear or adjust your clothes. To keep from feeling nervous, take action by doing something thoughtful. Also, remember that your open palms show your willingness to be open and honest, and in this case, passing out food and drink shows you to be caring as well.

Look for an Open Person

You've now learned how to make yourself approachable by having open body language. You can also use that information to look for people you can easily approach. Search for people who are already intently speaking to someone. Look for the ones who have their feet apart a few inches, rather than crossed, pressed together, or in a "cowboy" defensive stance (fourteen inches apart). It's easier to approach someone who is showing his or her palms while gesturing and smiling. If you are super shy, stand near someone who looks open and slowly mirror that person's posture. Research shows conversation is likely to ensue.

Go First

You can also introduce yourself. I know, I know, you're thinking, "Patti, you are insane. I hate to talk to people, and you want me to initiate? I'd rather stick a fork in my eye." Put down the fork. Research shows that when you initiate and move forward, you appear more confident to other people and they immediately feel more at ease. In addition, when they feel at ease, the comfort transfers back to you. A quick tip if you feel anxious: take one small step forward.

"May I Introduce...?"

Proper introductions help to establish rapport. You needn't get hung up on the rules below, but do consider them.

Authority, age, and gender determine who is introduced to whom. These also define whose name is said first. Always say the name of the most important person first, and then the name of the person being introduced to this important person. "President Kovak, may I introduce my client, Stephanie Jamison?" "Stephanie, this is our president, Nancy Kovak." or "Dr. Howard, may I introduce my youngest son, James?" "James, I would like you to meet Dr. Howard."

In your introduction, use the names and titles that the people you are introducing should use with each other.

Introduce people in the following order: younger to older, saying the older person's name first; nonofficial to official, saying the official person's name first; junior executive to senior executive, saying the senior executive's name first; colleague to customer; and so on.

Keep the introduction basic.

If the people you are introducing have the opportunity to speak to each other, ideally you should give them something to talk about. Provide some information about the people you are introducing to clarify your relationship with that person. For example, "Mom, I would like you to meet my friend Stella. She is the friend I trade dog-sitting chores with. Stella, this is my mother, Mrs. Patel, who lives in Florida."

If you don't remember someone's name, merrily say, "Forgive me, can you help me with your full name?" If you are with someone who doesn't introduce you to others, though you may want to elbow that person in the side and whisper, "Introduce me," try simply saying, "Hello my name is...You are?"

When you are introduced to someone, repeat the person's name and, yes, though it may sound dorky, it is appropriate to say, "It is a pleasure to meet you."[1]

(Go to www.snapfirstimpressions.com for a video of introductions. Watch the body language and listen to the wording and small talk of a first meeting.)

Introduce People to Each Other

This gives you something practical to do. Making introductions is appreciated by others, and it takes the pressure off you. As you stand and move to bring people together, you are creating a visual connection between you and other people in the room that makes you look powerful and popular. They see you move toward people and act as a connection, and they think, "Boy, she [or he] knows everyone."

Ask a Question, Then Relax and Listen

So much anxiety comes from not knowing what to do or how to do it well. One of the smartest things you can do at a party is ask a gentle question. It completely takes the talking pressure off you. You don't have to be witty and urbane to be a good listener. And everybody loves someone who really listens to them.

Nod Your Head

I love teaching men this simple listening body language cue. Men generally only nod their heads when they agree, while women nod to show they are listening. So guys, if you're interested, nod as you listen. Women love it.

—∾—

Even lifelong wallflowers who practice the above tips, I've found, turn into social butterflies who look forward to parties and meet-and-greet events of all kinds.

10. SNAP SUCCESS
EVERY DAY

Put Snap Know-How to Work
Each Day in Every Situation

You have learned that snap impressions are quick, powerful, and surprisingly accurate. We've seen that, although we are hardwired to give and receive them, we can get better at making snap impressions with practice. To wrap up, I have a "cheat sheet" that will help you always make your best possible snap. These tips for every situation apply to the four first-impression factors: credibility, likability, attractiveness, and power. Follow these tips and you'll always give a good first impression and connect well with others. When you first meet a person, these are the things to notice. And these are the same qualities that they will be looking for in you.

Start Powerfully

The primacy effect, according to persuasion research, indicates that the very first thing you say or do has the most power to capture attention and make a positive or negative impression. Be aware of how you enter any space, and focus your attention on others to make them feel comfortable. Prepare before you walk out your own door; if you don't have a full-length mirror, get one. Check yourself out from the tips of your toes to the top of your head. Darn it for being true, but attractiveness matters.

Step Forward

Move toward others with confidence. The most "honest" part of the body is that from the waist down. It is under the least conscious control and tends to be the first part of the body to respond to stress with the freeze-flight-fight-or-faint response. It is not surprising that, when we meet someone for the first time, or start an interaction, we feel a bit stressed. We may freeze up or step or lean back in retreat. To show you're credible, powerful, and confident, be the first to greet and make others feel welcome. Step, lean, or move forward slightly. Smile as you move, so the forward movement creates a likable and friendly impression.

Watch Your Stance and Posture

Hail to the Chief

Small nonverbal changes affect how others view us. For many years I have been analyzing political races and working as a political coach for people running for office and as a political commentator for the media. It's amazing how often the taller candidate and the one with the larger stance wins. When running for president for the first time, Barack Obama had a larger stance, stood up straighter, and had a more open posture than any of the other candidates. Stance affected the first impression he made on people — and perhaps the election results.

Stand with your weight evenly distributed on both feet. Balance centers you and actually makes you appear visually more balanced and attractive to others. In addition, power is communicated by taking up space. If your goal in your first impression is to look powerful or to feel strong and confident, the ideal for women is to stand with your feet six inches apart, and for men, six to eight inches apart. If you place your feet farther apart, you will tend to look defensive or aggressive. In fact, males will typically broaden their stance, placing their feet twelve inches or more apart, when they meet someone they feel threatened by or when they begin to debate or argue. So guys, watch your feet when you meet people who have more powerful positions or strong contrary opinions.

Face toward Others and Open Your Body Windows

Face people and give them your heart. Of course, you may want to take gender into consideration: men find that, in many interactions, standing or working side-by-side promotes buy-in and alliance. But in most cases, you'll want to meet and greet face-to-face so people see your open-window posture. The limbic brain reads this as "This person is confident and not guarding against attack." When you face your heart toward the person you're meeting, you're showing that you care.

Be Real in Facial Expressions and Body Movement

Be real and in the moment. The goal is to be present and to connect, rather than to be overly self aware. When I read body language in interrogation videos for law enforcement or for the media, I look for the natural synchronous nonverbal cues that show honesty. We feel an emotion, then we show it with our bodies and facial expression, and then we say it with our words. Remember to feel, show, say. For example, we naturally smile before we say, "I am having a great time," and grimace before we say, "I am mad." The time between actions may be only a millisecond, but for those listening and watching you, a variation in that order would be unsettling enough to affect the central nervous system.

　　When someone is lying, his timing is awkward and unnatural. This comes from his need to pause after a prepared lie and compose what he thinks is an appropriate gesture or expression. The nonverbal cues come late. So express yourself in a natural, synchronous way. In deception, or when a speaker is acting rather than feeling what he is saying in the moment, the beat is off. When you're speaking, first think of what you are feeling and what you want other people to feel.

Hands and Gestures

Do you remember the kid's game Simon Says? In an advanced version of the game, the leader says, for example, "Simon says touch your chin," but she instead touches her nose — and players often touch their noses, not their chins, in response. This reflects our tendency to believe and follow gestures more than the words people say. In fact, when a person's gestures and words differ, the listener will process the meaning of the gesture rather than the word.

This helps people understand us. Spencer Kelly, an associate professor of psychology at Colgate University, and Asli Özyürek and Eric Maris of Radboud University Nijmegen, the Netherlands, were interested in the interaction between speech and gesturing in public speaking and discovered that gesturing helps audiences learn the material more effectively if the gestures match the words.[1]

Your gestures are powerful. The most frequent question that I get when coaching someone who wants to improve his or her body language is "What do I do with my hands?" Remember, because the hands come out from the heart, they symbolically show our true feelings. Nervousness and anxiety show in our feet and hands. One of the reasons I love sharing how to give a great warm and confident handshake is because it gives you a powerful way to connect.

The location of your hands also affects your nonverbal behavior. Put your hands at your sides and your energy goes down. Your voice lowers and can become more monotonous, and you tend to move less and show fewer facial expressions. Bring your hands to the level of your waist, and you become calm and centered. Bring your hands up high to the level of your upper chest or above, and your voice goes up; you become more energized and animated. So change the location of your hands depending on how you want to feel and the impression you wish to make.

Have you ever known someone who "talked" with her hands? There are thousands of possible hand signals using different combinations of postures and arm, wrist, or finger movements. Gestures serve all sorts of communicative functions. They link and support the words we utter. Gestures can add meaning to something we say, give the feedback that we are listening, punctuate sentences, illustrate a point, give additional information, and more.

It may seem counterintuitive, but when you're nervous, gesturing meaningfully to illustrate your points can be helpful. Research on gesturing shows that the gesturing process actually helps us access more neural pathways in the brain, creating more connections and, consequently, smoothing out our speech and reducing pauses and vocal utterances such as "uh."

Right Hand, Good; Left Hand, Bad?

Does it matter to you and the person you're talking to which hand you gesture with? Well, in laboratory tests, right- and left-handed people "associate positive ideas like honesty and intelligence with their dominant side of space and negative ideas with their non-dominant side," says Daniel Casasanto of the Max Planck Institute for Psycholinguistics in Nijmegen, the Netherlands.[2] Casasanto and his coauthor, Kyle Jasmin, found that right-handed presidential candidates made a greater proportion of right-hand gestures when expressing positive ideas, and left-hand gestures when expressing negative thoughts. But the opposite was found for the left-handers, who favored their left hands for the positive and their right hands for the negative.

I tell my consulting clients who are nervous to try putting one hand in a pocket. For thirty years I have seen clients put their nondominant hands in their pockets and magically start to gesture with their dominant hands. Casasanto and Jasmin's data shows that people associate "good things with the side of their body they can use most fluently — dominant is fluent, and fluent is good."[3]

What to Do with Your Hands

In any interaction, ideally, keep your hands in view, rather than behind your back or in your pockets. When I train law enforcement officers in interrogation, I teach that one of the key places to look for deception is the palms of the hands. It is difficult to lie with the palms of your hands exposed.

If you must, you can put one hand in your pocket, but prepare ahead of time for this. Take all change and other objects out of your pockets, so you don't rattle them around and sound like Santa's sleigh. One stress-busting trick is to leave just a single nickel to squeeze.

Let your gestures flow naturally. They are a reflection of your authentic presence, of your personality flowing out, having an impact like waves on the shore.

Turn up the volume on your gestures. Practice being more animated, more expansive, more powerful. I'm barely five feet one, but I gesture like a giant. When people approach me after a speech, they are surprised to discover that I'm a munchkin.

Be aware of distracting repetitive hand motions, such as rubbing an earring or your mustache, twisting your hands, or pushing back your hair. We often use these comforting gestures while under stress, touching ourselves for reassurance. Practice minimizing these movements to increase your credibility and power.

Eye Contact

Eyes are designed to go toward movement so we can spy moving game and catch our supper. Since we take in 80 percent of our information via the eyes, monitoring others as we meet and converse is critical. It allows us to connect and be authentic.

The primary function of eye contact is to establish relationships. Our greatest fear in life is to be rejected. Each person with whom you make eye contact can feel accepted by you and connected to you, and the energy in that connection will assure you that you are accepted. Technology has reduced the amount of time we spend each day making eye contact. This makes it more important to make the effort to connect, and it also makes the results of eye contact much more powerful.

> ### Snap Finish
>
> A warm ending leaves a good impression. Some people say good-bye on the phone only halfheartedly, with a downward tone of voice or with a flippancy that can make you feel like you've wasted far too much of their time. Some people don't even bother to say good-bye, let alone "Nice talking to you" or "Thanks for your time" or "Let's talk again soon." Make sure you aren't one of these people. A warm, unrushed parting is as important as a warm, connecting greeting.

Looking at, and then looking away from, individuals allows us to process and access in-formation. Slowed blinking helps our overall thinking by giving us time to scan our brains for mental pictures and respond in a conversation or to an audience. Staring is not optimal, or natural, eye contact.

Remember the recency effect. People remember the last thing you say or do, and that affects your snap. The end of a greeting, meeting, or interaction is a time when many people get caught up in the rush to be off, and they forget to be present and honor the person or people in front of them. To create a powerful impact and connection, slow down and make significant, slightly lingering eye contact as you say good-bye.

—〰—

First, last, and foremost, remember that the greatest gift we can give other people is to truly understand them, to really see them. And that one of the greatest feelings we can experience is that of being truly understood and seen. My wish for you is that this book will help you to be truly seen and to give others the gift of truly seeing into their hearts.

ACKNOWLEDGMENTS

"How is the book coming?" has been the kind question my friends and family have asked me throughout the writing of this book, instead of "How are you?" A kind question, because all the people I love so much know this book has been like a dear child to me, and their question showed their support of my Times New Roman–printed baby so beautifully.

The first page I read in a book is the acknowledgments. It tells me much about the journey and heart of the author. I love to read how each book was born from the author but nurtured as well by the author's community of friends, family, and publishing guides. I am grateful to all of you for nurturing this book with me.

To the students I taught years ago in my nonverbal communication class at Florida State University, and on university campuses where I speak today: thank you for your boundless energy and enthusiasm. For my corporate clients and audiences through the years: thank you for your curiosity and questions. To my incredibly talented friends Pat MacEnulty, Steve Cohn, John Clark, and Mike Salone, who read the very first versions of this book: you gave from your heart, and I give to you a deep, from-the-heart thank-you.

To Jan and Robin, the best sisters any woman could have: thank you for your patience and love. To Mom: thanks for being the effervescent woman who enters any room, charms everybody present, and almost instantly learns the names of everyone there, the names of their children, and what is going on in their lives. And I thank my dad (now deceased), who taught us how to shake hands, tell stories, and laugh from the heart.

To my dear friends Judith, Steve D., Rodger, Jim, Enid, Bob, Renee, Morgan, and Maddison: thank you for all the love, laughter, and delicious home-cooked dinners you shared with me during the writing of this book. To my friends in our Thursday night discussion group: thank you. May we always have great questions from you as we "go around the table." An extra thanks to Craig, Cheryl, Jerry, Molly, Beth, Enid, Dorothy, and Yvette for helping me believe I could write a book people would want to read. To Jeff Kleinman, the nicest, funniest, most hardworking agent in the business: thank you. To the team at New World Library, including Kristen Cashman, Tracy Cunningham, Munro Magruder, Monique Muhlenkamp, Tona Myers, and Jonathan Wichmann: I thank you for your support. And to Georgia Hughes, the warmest, most thoughtful and long-viewed editor, I say, "Oh my goodness, thank you; it's a book!"

NOTES

Unless otherwise noted, all websites were accessed on February 16, 2012.

Chapter 1. Getting and Giving Snap Impressions

1. Janine Willis and Alexander Todorov, "First Impressions: Making Up Your Mind after a 100-Ms Exposure to a Face," *Psychological Science* 17 (July 2006): 592, http://pss.sagepub.com/content/17/7/592.short, accessed April 6, 2012.

2. Ibid.

3. Daniela Schiller, Jonathan Freeman, Jason Mitchell, James Uleman, and Elizabeth Phelps, "A Neural Mechanism of First Impressions," *Nature Neuroscience* 12 (2009): 508–14.

4. Nalini Ambady and Robert Rosenthal, "Thin Slices of Expressive Behavior as Predictors of Interpersonal Consequences," *Psychological Bulletin* 111, no. 2 (1992), www.scribd.com/doc/49151041/Ambady -Rosenthal-92-Thin-slices-of-expressive-behavior-as-predictors-of -interpersonal-consequences.

5. Depending on which personality aspects are measured and which method is used to check for accuracy, the degree of accuracy changes. For example, it is easier to identify characteristics like extroversion and competency, and more difficult to accurately access some others. See David C. Funder, "Errors and Mistakes: Evaluating the Accuracy of

Social Judgment," *Psychological Bulletin* 101, no. 1 (January 1987): 75–90, http://psy2.ucsd.edu/~mckenzie/FunderPsychBull1987.pdf; David A. Kenny and Linda Albright, "Accuracy in Interpersonal Perception: A Social-Relations Analysis," *Psychological Bulletin* 102, no. 3 (November 1987): 390–402; David A. Kenny, Linda Albright, Thomas E. Malloy, and Deborah A. Kashy, "Consensus in Interpersonal Perception: Acquaintance and the Big Five," *Psychological Bulletin* 116, no. 2 (September 1994): 245–58; Nalini Ambady and Robert Rosenthal, "Half a Minute: Predicting Teacher Evaluations from Thin Slices of Nonverbal Behavior and Physical Attractiveness," *Journal of Personality and Social Psychology* 64, no. 3 (March 1993): 431–41.

6. Philip Goldberg, *The Intuitive Edge: Understanding and Developing Intuition* (Los Angeles: Jeremy P. Tarcher, 1985), 36.

7. Ambady and Rosenthal, "Thin Slices of Expressive Behavior as Predictors of Interpersonal Consequences."

8. Gavin de Becker, *The Gift of Fear: And Other Survival Signals That Protect Us from Violence* (1997; repr., New York: Dell, 1999), 6, 11.

9. Daniel Amen, *Change Your Brain, Change Your Life* (New York: Three Rivers, 1999).

Chapter 2. What Happens in a Snap

1. James M. Kouzes and Barry Z. Posner, *Credibility: How Leaders Gain and Lose It, Why People Demand It* (San Francisco: Jossey-Bass, 1993).

2. David K. Berlo and James B. Lemert, "An Empirical Test of a General Construct of Credibility," paper presented to the Speech Association of America, New York, 1961.

3. Glenn E. Littlepage and Martin A. Pineault, "Detection of Deception of Planned and Spontaneous Communications," *Journal of Social Psychology* 125, no. 2 (1985): 195–201; Aldert Vrij, "The Impact of Information and Setting on Detection of Deception by Police Detectives," *Journal of Nonverbal Behavior* 18, no. 2 (June 1994): 117–36; Miron Zuckerman, Richard S. DeFrank, Judith A. Hall, Deborah T. Larrance, and Robert Rosenthal, "Facial and Vocal Cues of Deception and Honesty," *Journal of Experimental Social Psychology* 15, no. 4 (July 1979): 378–96.

4. Bella M. DePaulo, Amy L. Blank, Gregory W. Swaim, and Joan G. Hairfield, "Expressiveness and Expressive Control," *Personality and Social Psychology Bulletin* 18, no. 3 (June 1992): 276–85.

5. John Bowlby, *Maternal Care and Mental Health: A Report on Behalf of*

the World Health Organization (Geneva: World Heath Organization, 1952); Harry F. Harlow, "The Nature of Love," *American Psychologist* 13, no. 12 (1958); Ashley Montague, *Touching: The Human Significance of the Skin* (New York: Harper and Row, 1986).

6. Frank N. Willis and Helen K. Hamm, "The Use of Interpersonal Touch in Securing Compliance," *Journal of Nonverbal Behavior* 5, no. 1 (January 1, 1980).

7. Linda Albright, Thomas E. Malloy, Qi Dong, David A. Kenny, Xiaoyi Fang, Lynn Winquist, and Da Yu, "Cross-Cultural Consensus in Personality Judgments," *Journal of Personality and Social Psychology* 72, no. 3 (March 1997): 558–69; Leslie A. Zebrowitz, Karen Olson, and Karen Hoffman, "Stability of Babyfacedness and Attractiveness across the Life Span," *Journal of Personal and Social Psychology* 64, no. 3 (March 1993): 453–66.

8. Mel Gussow, "A Lustrous Pinnacle of Hollywood Glamour," *New York Times*, March 23, 1996, www.nytimes.com/2011/03/24/movies /elizabeth-taylor-obituary.html?pagewanted=all, accessed March 28, 2012.

9. Geoffrey Cowley, "The Biology of Beauty," *Newsweek*, June 3, 1996, 61.

10. Wake Forest University, "Rating Attractiveness: Consensus among Men, Not Women, Study Finds," *ScienceDaily*, June 26, 2009, www.science daily.com/releases/2009/06/090626153511.htm, accessed December 22, 2011.

11. Eve Tahmincioglu, "Power of Attraction Still Rules In Workplace," MSNBC.com, March 8, 2007, www.msnbc.msn.com/id/17369873 /ns/business-careers/t/power-attraction-still-rules-workplace/#. T5H4iu3_6ao.

12. Nicholas O. Rule and Nalini Ambady, "The Face of Success: Inferences from Chief Executive Officers' Appearance Predict Company Profits," *Psychological Science* 19, no. 2 (February 2008): 109–11.

13. Alan Feingold, "Good-Looking People Are Not What We Think," *Psychological Bulletin* 111, no. 2 (March 1992): 304–41.

14. Olivia A. O'Neill and Charles A. O'Reilly, "Reducing the Backlash Effect: Self-Monitoring and Women's Promotions," *Journal of Occupational and Organizational Psychology* 84, no. 4 (December 2011): 825–32.

15. "Snap Judgments about Candidates Are the Best Way to Pick Winners, Study Suggests," Dartmouth College Office of Public Affairs press release, November 6, 2006, www.dartmouth.edu/~news/releases /2006/11/06.html, accessed April 20, 2102.

Chapter 3. Meet and Greet

1. "Scientists Create Formula for the Perfect Handshake," July 14, 2010, www.chevrolet.co.uk/experience-chevrolet/news/2010/news /news-details2010-18.html.

2. Tomoya Kameia, Takao Tsudab, Shinya Kitagawab, Ken Naitoha, Koji Nakashimaa, and Toshio Ohhashi, "Physical Stimuli and Emotional Stress-Induced Sweat Secretions in the Human Palm and Forehead," *Analytica Chimica Acta* 365, no. 1–3 (June 1998).

3. Kathleen Deboer, *Gender and Competition: How Men and Women Approach Work and Play Differently* (Monterey, CA: Coaches Choice, 2004); Suzette Haden Elgin, *How to Disagree without Being Disagreeable: Getting Your Point Across with the Gentle Art of Verbal Self-Defense* (New York: John Wiley & Sons, 1997).

4. William F. Chaplin, Jeffrey B. Phillips, Jonathan D. Brown, Nancy R. Clanton, and Jennifer L. Stein, "Handshaking, Gender, Personality, and First Impressions," *Journal of Personality and Social Psychology* 79, no. 1 (July 2000): 110–17.

5. Charles M. Sennott, "Faith and Forgiveness in the Middle East," *Boston Globe*, April 4, 1999, magazine section, 12.

6. Jeff St. Cloud, "Secret Motorcycle Hand Greetings: Revealed!" *View from the Cloud*, August 22, 2006, www.viewfromthecloud.com/2006/08 /secret-motorcycle-hand-greetings.html.

7. Dan Cossins, "V for Victory," *BBC History Magazine*, Historyextra.com, www.historyextra.com/qa/v-victory, accessed April 20, 2012.

8. Wikipedia, "Peace Symbols," http://en.wikipedia.org/wiki/Peace _symbol, accessed January 16, 2012.

9. "Michelle Obama's G20 Faux Pas Brings Out Queen's Touchy-Feely Side," *Guardian* (UK), April 2, 2009, www.guardian.co.uk/world /blog/2009/apr/02/michelle-obama-queen-hug?INTCMP=SRCH, accessed March 30, 2012.

Chapter 4. The Face of First Impressions

1. Mark Knapp and Judith Hall, *Nonverbal Communication in Human Interaction* (Belmont, CA: Wadsworth, 2006).

2. Martin Rolfs, Donatas Jonikaitis, Heiner Deubel, Patrick Cavanagh. "Predictive Remapping of Attention across Eye Movements," *Nature Neuroscience* 14, no. 2 (2011): 252–56.

3. Steven A. Beebe, "Effects of Eye Contact, Posture and Vocal Inflection

upon Credibility and Comprehension," study prepared at the University of Miami, 1976, www.eric.ed.gov/PDFS/ED144121.pdf.

4. Roel Vertegaal and Yaping Ding, "Explaining Effects of Eye Gaze on Mediated Group Conversations: Amount or Synchronization?" paper presented at the Association for Computing Machinery Conference on Computer Supported Cooperative Work, New Orleans, LA, November 16–20, 2002, www.sciencedaily.com/releases/2002/11 /021122073858.htm.

5. Yin Wang, Richard Ramsey, and Antonia Hamilton, "The Control of Mimicry by Eye Contact Is Mediated by Medial Prefrontal Cortex," *Journal of Neuroscience* 31, no. 33 (August 17, 2011): 12001–10, www .sciencedaily.com/releases/2011/08/110816171428.htm.

6. Louann Brizendine, *The Female Brain* (New York: Three Rivers Press, 2007), 15.

7. Alan Fogel and Angela Uchoa Branco, "Meta-communication as a Source of Indeterminism in Relationship Development," in Alan Fogel, Maria C. D. P. Lyra, and Jaan Valsiner, eds., *Dynamics and Indeterminism in Developmental and Social Processes* (Mahwah, NJ: Erlbaum, 1997), 68. In addition to the paper cited above, much of Alan Fogel's groundbreaking research in the field has informed my conclusions here; see http://utah.academia.edu/AlanFogel/Papers for more information. Also, see Ruth Feldman, Charles W. Greenbaum, and Nurit Yirmiya, "Mother–Infant Affect Synchrony as an Antecedent of the Emergence of Self-Control," *Developmental Psychology* 35, no. 1 (January 1999): 223.

8. J. J. Tecce, "Body Language in 2004 Presidential Debates," www.social-engineer.org/wiki/archives/EyeMovement/Eye Movement-2004ElectionAnalysis.htm.

9. Adam Kendon and Mark Cook, "The Consistency of Gaze Pattern in Social Interaction," *British Journal of Psychology* 60, no. 4 (1969): 481–94.

10. Leslie Holmes, "The Effects of Interviewees' Nonverbal Behavior on Interviewers' Evaluations during a Selection Interview," PhD diss., January 1, 1983, University of Nebraska at Lincoln, http://digital commons.unl.edu/dissertations/AAI8318659.

11. Karl Grammer, Wulf Schiefenhovel, Margret Schleidt, Beatrice Lorenz, and Irenäus Eibl-Eibesfeldt, "Patterns on the Face: The Eyebrow Flash in Crosscultural Comparison," *Ethology* 77, no. 4 (1988): 279–99.

12. Bhismadev Chakrabarti and Simon Baron-Cohen, "Variation in the Human Cannabinoid Receptor CNR1 Gene Modulates Gaze Duration

for Happy Faces," *Molecular Autism* 2 (June 29, 2011), www.molecular autism.com/content/2/1/10.

13. Lane Strathearn, Jian Li, Peter Fonagy, and P. Read Montague, "What's in a Smile?: Maternal Brain Responses to Infant Facial Cues," *Pediatrics* 122, no. 1 (July 2008): 40–51.

14. Marco Iacoboni, "The Mirror Neuron Revolution: Explaining What Makes Humans Social," *Scientific American*, July 1, 2008, www.scientific american.com/article.cfm?id=the-mirror-neuron-revolut.

15. Pierre Kaldy, "Born to Smile: New Evidence That Laughing and Smiling Begin in the Womb," November 25, 2011, Worldcrunch, www .worldcrunch.com/born-smile-new-evidence-laughing-and-smiling -begin-womb/4125?device=auto.

16. Deborah Blum, "Face It!," *Psychology Today*, September 1998, www.psychologytoday.com/articles/200909/face-it.

17. Tonic.com, "Brain Processes Happy Faces Fastest," June 23, 2009, www.tonic.com/p/our-brains-process-happy-expressions-more -rapidly-than-sad-or-angry-ones, accessed December 7, 2011.

18. Paul Ekman, Richard J. Davidson, and Wallace V. Friesen, "The Duchenne Smile: Emotional Expression and Brain Physiology," *Journal of Personality and Social Psychology* 58, no. 2 (1990).

19. Jennifer Viegas, "Smiling? You Can Hear It in the Voice," January 3, 2008, Discovery News, http://dsc.discovery.com/news/2008/01/03 /smile-communication.html.

20. James M. Dabbs, "Testosterone, Smiling, and Facial Appearance," *Journal of Nonverbal Behavior* 21, no. 1 (1997): 45–55.

Chapter 5. Connections in a Snap

1. Sigal G. Barsdale, "The Ripple Effect: Emotional Contagion and Its Influence on Group Behavior," *Administrative Science Quarterly* 47, 644–75, www.management.wharton.upenn.edu/barsade/docs /Barsade_Emotional_Contagion_in_Groups.pdf.

2. Elaine Hatfield, John T. Cacioppo, and Richard L. Rapson, "Emotional Contagion," *Current Directions in Psychological Sciences* 2 (1993): 2, www.elainehatfield.com/ch50.pdf.

3. Jean Decety and William Ickes, eds., *The Social Neuroscience of Empathy* (Cambridge, MA: MIT Press, 2009), 19.

4. Carolyn Coakley and Andrew Wolvin, "Listening in the Educational Environment," in Deborah Borisoff and Michael Purdy, *Listening in*

Everyday Life (Lanham, MD: University Press of America, 1991; second edition, 1997), 179–212.

Chapter 6. Your Techno Impression

1. Steven Rosenbaum, "As Email Wheezes toward the Grave, We Contemplate a DNR," *Fast Company*, Expert Blog, December 5, 2011, www.fastcompany.com/1799096/Can-We-Save-Email-Should-We.

2. Sara Radicati, ed., *Email Statistics Report*, 2009–2013 (Radicati Group, 2010), summary available at www.radicati.com/wp/wp-content /uploads/2011/05/Email-Statistics-Report-2011-2015-Executive -Summary.pdf.

3. Linda Stone, "Continuous Partial Attention," http://lindastone.net /qa/continuous-partial-attention.

4. Gary Small and Gigi Vorgan, "Your iBrain: How Technology Changes the Way We Think," *Scientific American* (October 8, 2008), www .scientificamerican.com/article.cfm?id=your-ibrain.

5. Anna T. Collins, "Texting: The New Prose, or: What the QWERTY Does It All Mean?" *MiamiArtzine.com*, January 30, 2011, www.miamiartzine .com/issue_main.cfm?btitle=textingandid=1499andkeyx=678117801, accessed March 29, 2012.

6. Larry Carlat, "Confessions of a Tweeter," *New York Times*, November 11, 2011, www.nytimes.com/2011/11/13/magazine/confessions-of-a-tweeter .html.

7. Kevin W. Rockmann and Gregory B. Northcraft, "To Be or Not to Be Trusted: The Influence of Media Richness on Defection and Deception," *Organizational Behavior and Human Decision Processes* 107, no. 2 (November 2008), www.sciencedirect.com/science/article/pii /S0749597808000149, accessed March 29, 2012.

Chapter 7. How You Look to Others in a Snap

1. Mary Madden and Amanda Lenhart, "Online Dating," Pew Internet and American Life Project, March 5, 2006, www.pewinternet.org /~/media/files/reports/2006/pip_online_dating.pdf.pdf, accessed March 3, 2012; Thomas Lewis, Fari Amini, and Richard Lannon, *A General Theory of Love* (New York: Random House, 2000), 85.

2. Don E. Hamachek, *Encounters with Others: Interpersonal Relationships and You* (New York: Holt, Rinehart and Winston, 1982).

Chapter 8. Work World Snaps

1. The key points of this list were summarized from the following research sources, all of which were accessed February 15, 2012: Carole Martin, "Boost Your Hiring IQ: Take the Manager's Hiring IQ Test," www.boostyourhiringiq.com; Citynews.ca staff, "The Top Mistakes Job Interviewers Are Making," *City News Toronto*, August 15, 2007, www.citytv.com/toronto/citynews/life/money/article /15735--the-top-mistakes-job-interviewers-are-making; Scott Erker, PhD, and Kelli Buczynski, "Are You Failing the Interview?: 2009 Survey of Global Interviewing Practices and Perceptions," www.ddiworld.com /DDIWorld/media/trend-research/are-you-failing-the-interview _tr_ddi.pdf; Kelli Buczynski, "Getting the Right Candidate to Say Yes," www.imakenews.com/ddi/e_article001281599.cfm?x=b11,0.

Chapter 9. Your Social Snap

1. For more on etiquette, see Sharon L. Cohen, eHow, "How to Make Proper Introductions," www.ehow.com/how_2352298_make-proper -introductions.html; Advanced Etiquette, "Proper Introductions," July 2003, www.advancedetiquette.com/newsletter/july_issue.htm; Essortment, "What Is the Proper Way to Make an Introduction?" www.essortment.com/proper-way-make-introduction-59623.html.

Chapter 10. Snap Success Every Day

1. Spencer Kelly, Asli Özyürek, and Eric Maris, "Two Sides of the Same Coin: Speech and Gesture Mutually Interact to Enhance Comprehension," *Psychological Science* 21, no. 2 (February 2010): 260–67.

2. D. Casasanto and K. Jasmin, "The Hands of Time: Temporal Gestures in English Speakers," read in draft form, in *Cognitive Linguistics*, February 2012.

3. Ibid.

INDEX

ABOUT THE AUTHOR

Called "the gold standard of body language experts" by the *Washington Post*, and credited in the *New York Times* with bringing body language to national consciousness, Patti Wood researches and consults on first impressions, body language, and nonverbal communication. Patti Wood, MA, CSP, speaks to Fortune 500 companies, national associations, judges, and law enforcement organizations. You can see her on CNN, *Fox News*, PBS, *Good Morning America*, the Discovery Channel, *Dr. Drew*, Bravo, the History Channel, *Nancy Grace*, *Entertainment Tonight*, *Inside Edition*, *Prime News*, *In Session*, True TV, Fox Business Network, and other national news and entertainment programs. Her insights on body language and her readings of politicians, criminal suspects, and celebrities are quoted in publications such as the *Wall Street Journal*, *Psychology Today*, *Bloomberg Businessweek*, *Fortune*, *Esquire*, *Sports Illustrated*, *Cosmopolitan*, *USA Today*, *US Weekly*, and *People*, and on Aol.com, *Huffington Post*, and *The Week*. She lives near Atlanta, Georgia, and can be reached for media interviews and to be booked for speeches and workshops through her website, www.pattiwood.net.

NEW WORLD LIBRARY is dedicated to publishing books and other media that inspire and challenge us to improve the quality of our lives and the world.

We are a socially and environmentally aware company, and we strive to embody the ideals presented in our publications. We recognize that we have an ethical responsibility to our customers, our staff members, and our planet.

We serve our customers by creating the finest publications possible on personal growth, creativity, spirituality, wellness, and other areas of emerging importance. We serve New World Library employees with generous benefits, significant profit sharing, and constant encouragement to pursue their most expansive dreams.

As a member of the Green Press Initiative, we print an increasing number of books with soy-based ink on 100 percent postconsumer-waste recycled paper. Also, we power our offices with solar energy and contribute to nonprofit organizations working to make the world a better place for us all.

Our products are available
in bookstores everywhere.
For our catalog, please contact:

New World Library
14 Pamaron Way
Novato, California 94949

Phone: 415-884-2100 or 800-972-6657
Catalog requests: Ext. 50
Orders: Ext. 52
Fax: 415-884-2199
Email: escort@newworldlibrary.com

To subscribe to our electronic newsletter, visit
www.newworldlibrary.com